Revelation and Redemption

A SKETCH OF THE THEOLOGY OF ST. JOHN

Revelation
and Redemption

A SKETCH OF THE THEOLOGY OF ST. JOHN

by DR. WILLIAM GROSSOUW
University of Nijmegen
The Netherlands

Translated and edited from the Dutch by
REV. MARTIN W. SCHOENBERG, O.S.C.

THE NEWMAN PRESS
WESTMINSTER, MARYLAND
1955

Originally published as *Het Christendom van Johannes*
by Uitgeverij Het Spectrum, Utrecht, Holland

Nihil obstat: ALOYSIUS J. MEHR, O.S.C., *Censor Deputatus*
Imprimi potest: LAWRENCE J. KERICH, O.S.C., *Vicar General*
Imprimatur: LOUIS B. KUCERA, D.D., *Bishop of Lincoln*

March 1, 1955

Library of Congress Catalog Card Number: 55-8010
Copyright, 1955, by THE NEWMAN PRESS
Printed in the United States of America

Contents

❖❖❖❖❖❖❖❖❖

Contents

Introduction

Introduction

◆◆◆◆◆◆◆◆◆

THIS little book is not an introduction to the
fourth Gospel in the ordinary sense of the
word. It was my hope and intention to bring the
Catholic of today into contact with the Johannine
realm of thought. To do this it was above all necessary to present an exposition of John's manner of
thinking and writing and the peculiar character of
his Gospel, as is done in the first chapter. What follows after that is really a theology of St. John. I
have tried to lead the reader *into* the sanctum of the
beloved disciple's thought, not merely to bring him
to the threshold and then abandon him there. The
customary introductions to the Bible and to its sep-
arate parts do admittedly contain much necessary,
albeit rather arid, information worth knowing about
the personality of the writer, the content and division of his work, the date of its composition, etc.
Ordinarily, however, all these do not bring us much
closer to the essence and the spirit of the book as a
whole; frequently they serve to repel the layman

rather than to entice him to further consideration of the matter. For this reason they have been omitted here. They can readily be found in the well-known introductions to the various editions of the Gospels.[1]

A rudimentary knowledge of these things is pre-supposed in this little work—as also the Catholic dogmatic teaching on the inspiration and the apostolic origin of the Johannine writings, and above all, a serious and constant reading of the text itself. Without this personal effort, without a certain famil-iarity with the Gospel and the First Epistle of St. John, this presentation will completely miss its pur-pose. For this book intends only to serve the text as faithfully as possible; it is not meant to be apologetic, oratorical, or moralizing for its own sake.

In order to explain and to complete the teaching of the fourth Gospel constant reference is made to the First Epistle of St. John. One may perhaps frown upon this method of procedure, since the point of view and the circumstances of the Epistle are not identical to those of the Gospel. But the advantages in comparing the two far outweigh the disadvan-tages just mentioned. Furthermore, these disadvan-

---

[1] All standard modern editions of the Bible have such introduc-tory notes: e.g., the Confraternity edition of the New Testament, Paterson, 1941; Spencer's translation of the New Testament, New York, 1937; The Westminster Version of the New Testament (small edition) London, 1947; the Kleist-Lilly translation of the New Testament, Milwaukee, 1954. (Translator's note)

tages are quite theoretical. Since the Apocalypse is a writing of an entirely different kind, it has not been considered.[2] Such quotations from the Bible which are not accompanied by any further specifications, e.g., 1:14, are taken from the Gospel of St. John. Others which are preceded by the Roman numeral I, e.g., I 2:2, refer to the First Epistle.

[2] The author here mentions the Dutch translations of the Bible which he used for his quotations from the Sacred Scriptures. For the English translation I have used the Confraternity edition of the New Testament for quotations from the New Testament, and the standard Douay Version, published by P. J. Kenedy & Sons, New York, for quotations from the Old Testament. (Translator's note)

Revelation and Redemption

A SKETCH OF THE THEOLOGY OF ST. JOHN

CHAPTER ONE

The End and the Means

✧✧✧✧✧✧✧✧✧

I. The Purpose and the Leading Ideas

John's purpose: the faith and the life of his readers— the fourth Gospel, written as the fruit of the fullness of religious experience —the one theme: Christ, the Son of God— the leading thoughts with their logical consequences.

IN ORDER to understand a writer and to judge him rightly one must know his purpose in writing. This is all the more true when treating authors of antiquity, whose literary methods differ considerably from ours. Concerning St. John's purpose in writing the fourth Gospel, we are luckily not groping in the dark, for at the end of his work the Apostle himself indicates his intention: "Many other signs also Jesus worked in the sight of his disciples, which are not written in this book. But these are

1

written that you may believe that Jesus is the Christ, the Son of God, and that believing you may have life in his name" (20:30–31). These simple words are very important to anyone wishing to understand St. John. He lets it be known definitely that he had a specific purpose in mind, a purpose which set strict limitations upon his work. It was not his intention to narrate all he knew about Jesus. He purposely omitted many signs which Jesus worked, even though he was an eye-witness to them (19:35; 21:24) and was consequently certain of them.

Thus it follows that he was not impelled to write by the inquisitiveness which prompts the modern historian; the Gospel is not a repertory of all the things worth knowing about his hero. One might sooner suppose that such was St. Luke's intention, since he avows that he strove after a certain amount of completeness, but that he was not an eye-witness to the incidents he narrates (Lk. 1:3). On the contrary, St. John indicates in a positive manner the goal he intends to reach by the selection of the words and deeds of Jesus which he does narrate. This goal is the *faith* of his readers and the *life* which they will obtain through faith (20:30–31). These two words place us, as it were with one stroke, in the very center of the Johannine realm of ideas. By his writings John seeks to arouse a perfect and profound faith, such a faith as will not only lead to *eternal life* but which is eternal life already begun.

The Apostle desires to let his readers share his own view of Christ, his own experience of Christ. He wishes to introduce them to the motivation and starting point of his writing. This is not so much the narration of, as a testimony to, a living and deep and eternal reality, to the only reality that still exists for him. Listen to the words of the Prologue as even now they ring with rapturous enthusiasm: "The Word was made flesh, and dwelt among us. And we saw his glory—glory as of the only-begotten of the Father—full of grace and of truth." The opening lines of the Epistle testify to the same experience: "I write of what was from the beginning, what we have heard, what we have seen with our eyes, what we have looked upon and our hands have handled; of the Word of Life. . . . What we have seen and have heard we announce to you, in order that you also may have fellowship with us. . . ." A document which has its origin in such a plenitude of experience and which is intended as a means to enable others to share this experience must not be classified as being purely historical in point of view. However, this is not to say that it does not have a historical basis, or that it is not historically true.

The intention of the fourth Gospel is a practical-religious one, not an objective-historical one in the modern sense of the term. John does not take a disinterested view of his subject matter—how could he? In John's view, Christ is not an object of knowledge. For him, Christ is not an object at all; rather He is "My God and my All," the Light and the Source of his own life, the Truth whom he has seen, and who has taken complete possession of his spirit. One might call his Gospel biased; but one must then add that it has a bias which the author himself points out, a bias which the historicity—the truth of the narration—urgently demands.

In the Epilogue (20:30–31) John also tells us the content of the faith which has been the theme of his Gospel, and which he has striven to arouse in his readers. It is Jesus, who is the Christ, the Son of God. Even these words can be fully comprehended only in the light of the whole Gospel. Let us affirm for the time being that the fourth Gospel is Christocentric. Everything revolves about this one central point, around the person of Christ. The other Gospels, of course, are also occupied with Jesus, but not in the same measure as that of John. John knows only one theme: Jesus, as the Christ, the Son of God. His intent is not merely to point out that Jesus is the Messias who was announced by the Old Testament or to *prove* that He is the Son of God, but

4

he wishes to bear witness to Him. He is determined to make his readers see, feel, and experience as far as is possible the supreme and only adequate revelation of God, as it appeared in the incarnate Logos, the glory of God which was manifested to him in Jesus. Whoever knows Christ in this manner possesses life; this is what constitutes the essence of Christendom. All the rest flows from this by virtue of intrinsic necessity. John thus reaches out to the most profound and ultimate basis, to the very center of the Christian mode of existence: the person of Christ as the revelation of God, the meeting and the union of the spirit of man with this divine reality in faith.

The writer pursues the program contained in these verses with incredible logic. This lends the Gospel a unity of concept and a conciseness which give the reader a profound impression of a religious experience. A few examples will suffice to show to what extent the four principal ideas—*faith, life, the Christ, the Son of God*—pervade and dominate the whole structure of the work even to its least details. This is immediately apparent in the Prologue. But even in other passages, which are apparently less adaptable, these ideas form the definitive character. The first narrative that follows on the Prologue tells of the witnessing of John the Baptist (1:19–

34). He steps forth not in his own behalf, but only in his function as voice, as the witness for Christ. His very first word is noteworthy in this regard: "I am not the Christ," as is also his last: "I have seen and have borne witness that this is the Son of God." This is the final impression which the reader must retain from this account. He does not learn what happened to John himself or what result these words had among the religious authorities of Jerusalem. The writer has narrated enough to accomplish his purpose; the rest is of no importance. A similar phenomenon can be ascertained in the episode of Nicodemus. With the pronouncement which Jesus makes about Himself (3:13ff.) John has ascended the heights which are his proper spiritual atmosphere. And there he remains (3:16–21). Notice the recurrent usage of the terms *faith, love, Son of God, Only-begotten.* Nicodemus has completely disappeared from the sphere of his vision so that one might almost consider him a symbol, if his name did not occur twice later in the Gospel.

John is not always dominated so strongly by his religious pragmatism; however, the reader can easily ascertain for himself that it has its influence throughout the entire Gospel. One need only compare the account of the Passion as it is given by John and by the other Evangelists. His religious pragmatism determines the choice of matter as well as the order and the form under which it is presented. His material differs to a great extent from that of the Synoptics; the greatest divergence is found in the fact that, drawing on his own personal memoirs, which are strongly colored by his personal dispositions and character, he is less restricted than the older Evangelists, who in the final analysis were dependent on the early-Christian catechesis. Writing at a later period, in a more developed condition of Christianity and for well-informed Christians, John impresses his own personality on his Gospel much more than do the Synoptics. But his personality is in turn stamped with the seal of Christ—of Christ, as John was privileged to see Him.

II. The Johannine Manner of Thought and Expression

The poverty of his language—his manner of thinking—representations rather than concepts—figurative language—testimony in place of proof.

THE real difficulty which the modern reader experiences with the fourth Gospel has its root in St. John's manner of thinking and taking notice of things. St. John does not think and express himself as we do. The present problem touches upon the formal aspect of the Gospel, if one wishes to put it that way, whereas the preceding section treated of its material element. The difficulties we encounter when reading St. John are not those which ordinarily make it difficult to read an ancient document and which can be overcome with the aid of a good philological commentary. St. John's language is utterly simple; we might even call it poor. Of all the Evangelists his vocabulary is the most limited. He prefers *ordinary* words. He does not know the artificially compounded terms which abound in the Greek language or the Attic classicisms in which the Hellenistic St. Luke occasionally delights. He is unfamiliar with the forced phrases which Paul coins in moments of intense spiritual emotion, and even with the picturesque expressions of the unlettered Mark. St. John uses comparatively few words; he clings to his favorite terms, which recur constantly. There is even less difficulty because of involved and intricate constructions. If one may say so, St. John's syntax is not very Greek. This Semite is not acquainted with fine periods, the crowning glory of Attic prose, or with the conjunctions so characteristic of the Greek language. Ninety per cent of the varied modes of expression which this beautiful language offers are left unused. In St. John one finds little of that marvelous classic medium so suitable for expressing subtle shades of thought and for registering the most delicate emotions of the soul. John's language and style are rather characterized by a solemn monotony, which is admirably suited to his subject, but which does not impede the formation of a just and convenient concept of his Gospel. Neither is the special difficulty in understanding his Gospel caused by the fact that it is an ancient writing. If one gives an educated man a good translation of Thucydides or of Plutarch, supplemented with a brief explanation and suitable notes, he has no difficulty in following the development of thought, because their manner of thinking is ultimately the same as ours.

This is not the case when reading St. John. One

example out of many will suffice to illustrate the point. When Jesus had promised the Eucharistic bread, He spoke thus: " 'The bread that I will give is my flesh for the life of the world.' The Jews on that account argued with one another, saying, 'How can this man give us his flesh to eat?' Jesus therefore said to them, 'Amen, amen, I say to you, unless you eat the flesh of the Son of Man, and drink his blood, you shall not have life in you. He who eats my flesh and drinks my blood has life everlasting and I will raise him up on the last day. For my flesh is food indeed, and my blood is drink indeed. He who eats my flesh, and drinks my blood, abides in me and I in him' " (6:52–57). The only point which is immediately and absolutely clear to us in this short passage is the objection of the Jews. As far as our sentiment is concerned, there is something wanting in Jesus' answer. We ask ourselves whether it is really an answer. It seems rather that Jesus merely ignores the difficulty and is content to repeat His assertion in slightly different words. The subsequent verses all develop the same thought, *but not in a manner familiar to us*. It is the same thought that constantly recurs, somewhat modified, but always in its totality. The thought does not advance; it appears to be standing still. Or more accurately, the progression of his thought is not linear, but *concentric,* re-

10

volving spirally about the one central point without ever fully attaining it.

Our mode of thinking, and I mean here the process which we call reasoning, the concatenation of judgments, is either psychological or logical. Most often it is the latter, which means that in its last analysis our thinking is based on the laws of Aristotelian logic. Western thought and Greek thought are basically alike. This is why a writing from classical antiquity is immediately intelligible to us. This mode of thought is conceptual, abstract, syllogistic, dialectic. It is a process of reasoning, of demonstration, of explicit or implicit linking of syllogisms. The thought advances in a direct line by incorporating new ideas and arranging them under the major proposition. It develops progressively and gradually reaches its completion. It is comparable to a road that has been mapped out from a starting point, with sundry stopping places and a final goal.

John's manner of thought differs from ours in two points which are necessarily connected. First (I), he does not work with abstract concepts, but with *representations* which when compared with ours have not lost their visible and concrete aspect. His thought is primarily a contemplation, a spiritual observation, an immediate intuition of the living reality. We say: God is unlimited perfection. John

11

says: "God is light, and in him is no darkness" (I 1:5). Our theology uses the formula: God is the source of all grace, an image which is no longer an image. But in the Gospel of St. John, Jesus says: "I am the vine, you are the branches" (15:5). It is evident that this utterance is not to be taken as a definition or as an exact determination of a specific essence. Neither is it a figure of speech (metaphor, mentonymy, allegory etc.) in our use of the term. The first point is clear.

The second perhaps may not be, since modern exegesis commonly treats such expressions as figures of speech. We really have only two kinds of figures of speech: those which serve to illustrate an assertion, and poetical expressions which serve to describe an object graphically. We are inclined to look upon St. John's imagery as figures of speech wherein the third term (the *tertium comparationis*) alone has a role, and which can be represented and solved with the mathematical formula a:b—c:d, or, Jesus bears a similar relationship to His disciples as the vine does to the branches. It is true that by such artifices we approximate what John had in mind, but we never fully attain it. Otherwise why does he have Jesus say elsewhere: "I am the *true* vine"? [1]

[1] One need only consult the commentary of St. Augustine (Migne, P.L., 35, 1839; *Tractatus in Johannem 80*). Augustine

What John really wants to say may be put something like this: that organic unity and that common life which exist between a vine and its branches, which we consider as a natural phenomenon, are even much more real in the relationship that exists between Jesus and His disciples, and are actually only fully realized in this latter relationship. The vine is really only a *symbol,* a sensible representation of the supreme truth of the latter comparison. And yet even this ponderous paraphrase is a paraphrase, no more. Nor can this manner of speech be simply reduced to poetical imagery. It is not a medium for beautiful and picturesque expression, though it may possibly be granted that the poet is more apt to understand the fourth Gospel than the philosopher.

How strange our ordinary, lifeless concepts are to St. John becomes obvious in precisely those places where his thought seems to be contained in abstract formulas without any figurative elements. There is great danger of misunderstanding a passage such as 18:37–38 and of taking it in a philosophical or

asks how Christ can call Himself the *true* vine, since this is merely a figure of speech (*sic enim dicitur vitis per similitudinem, non per propietatem* . . .). In answer he refers to Jer. 2:21, where Jahweh addresses the people of Israel in the following manner: "Yet I planted thee a chosen vineyard, all true seed: how then art thou turned unto me into that which is good for nothing. O strange vineyard?" But Christ, says St. Augustine, is the good vineyard which brings forth only good fruit. It is evident that this is merely a subterfuge.

13

idealistic sense. What sounds more abstract than the question of Pilate: "What is truth?" Could one not consider the words Jesus has just pronounced as the declaration of some vague humanitarian principle? The second part of the preceding verse already warns us against such an interpretation: "This is why I was born, and why I have come into the world, to bear witness to the truth. Everyone who is of the truth hears my voice." It is clear to anyone who has even the most superficial knowledge of the fourth Gospel that this truth is not the universal relationship between a being and an intellect, or of any other logical or ontological concept of truth one may cherish. On the contrary, it is the living religious truth, the concrete revelation of God in Christ. For the same reason such an expression as "God is love" (I 4:8) may not be considered as a definition. In John's view God is not the basic principle of some cosmic movement, the Platonic *eros,* or whatever you will. The Apostle's thought does not move among these categories. God is *agapē* (love), not ordinary love, but that unique movement of love in the bosom of the divinity, that love of the Father and the Son which manifests itself externally by the mission of the Only-begotten into this world and His deliverance unto death "for the life of the world"— a movement shared with the individual Christian and

14

which, consummated by this sharing, returns to its starting point, God.

These graphic representations, to put it briefly, are a necessary consequence of the peculiar logic of John's thinking. Here we have the second difference (II) between John's mode of thought and ours. John does not reason; he "bears witness," he affirms. He does not prove, he draws no conclusions, he does not lead the reader by gradual deductions toward the comprehension of the whole, his thought does not develop by adding the different parts to constitute the entirety. Instead, he places his reader directly in front of the reality which he himself was privileged to see. This supernatural reality is the center whence all his ideas originate. All his judgments move around this one central point (concentric thinking), constantly endeavoring to approach even closer and to grasp it (spiral thinking). This hidden and mysterious center is no other than Christ. Hence the reality which must find expression in the passage quoted above (6:52 ff.) is this: Christ, the Bread of Life. It is already fully contained in v. 52, and the movement of the thought around this central point is maintained in the following verses, in spite of the objections of the Jews. There is also a certain development in the thought. Thus the notion *life* in v. 54 is clarified by the teaching of the resurrection of the body in

15

v. 55. Still, the latter verses do not add anything substantially new to those which preceded.

It is in this trait of John's thought that the above mentioned peculiarities of language and style have their origin. These peculiarities include his poverty of ideas, the simplicity of sentence construction, the numerous repetitions, the elevated monotony of his style. Mention must be made in particular here of two phenomena. John's representations are *open;* they are not sharply delineated. If one may so express it, they have something vague, something mobile about them when contrasted with purely abstract concepts. As illustration one may read a passage such as 3:19–21, "Now this is the judgment: The light has come into the world, yet men have loved the darkness rather than the light, for their works were evil. For everyone who does evil hates the light, and does not come to the light, that his deeds may not be exposed. But he who does the truth comes to the light that his deeds may be made manifest, for they have been performed in God." Does *light* signify Christ, Christianity, moral goodness, or the light of day? When we begin to analyze these verses according to our own fashion, we almost have the queer feeling that a joke is being played on us. The precise content of the word *light* constantly escapes us; we are always on unsteady ground. Our

concept *animal* is perfectly outlined and differen-
diated from the concept *plant* or *man*. Such is not the
case with the concept *light* in St. John, because it is
not a concept; it is an image, a representation of a
complex totality.

Another characteristic which St. John's ideas
often possess is *absoluteness*. Because they are significations of the supreme reality and of the center
of all things, Christ, they have absolute value.
For the very same reason they may often be used
interchangeably, for instance: life, light, truth.
It is a matter of utmost importance that we be fully
aware of this distinctive method of thought and expression when we begin reading the fourth Gospel.
We must constantly renounce our own cherished
modes of thinking. We must endeavor to grasp John
from within, to penetrate the visible and concrete
element of his representations, to permit ourselves
to be swept along by the movement of his thought.[2]

[2] The remarks made here apply primarily to the words of Jesus
and to the personal observations of the Evangelist. On first sight
the narrative sections appear much more easily understandable to
us, but in the last analysis their manner of expression is governed
by the same laws.

Of less importance here is the question: To which factors must
we ascribe these characteristics of the Johannine manner of thinking? To a certain extent they may certainly be attributed to the
Semitic temperament of the author. Everyone knows how concrete
and plastic is the language of the Psalms and of the Old Testament prophets. Abstract language seems foreign to the Semitic.
However, the other writers of the New Testament, with the exception of Luke, were also Semites; yet there exists a great difference

III. The Specific Character of the Fourth Gospel

The fourth Gospel not history in the technical sense—its relationship with the Synoptics—the problem of the words of Jesus —symbolism and realism—John, the theologian.

THE word gospel makes many think of a narrative of the life of Jesus, and consequently of history. Is the Gospel of St. John properly history in this sense? It has already been hinted above that the answer to this question cannot be given unconditionally in the affirmative. It is evident that we may not call the Gospel of St. John history in the modern scientific sense. Nor does it treat history as did some of the best historical writers of antiquity, such as Thucydides. Even among the writers of the New Testament there are those whose work is of a more historical nature than is John's. The reason for this is that the idea of pure history is lacking in St. John.[3]

between them and St. John. Hence one may conclude that personal factors have played their role, and reference is ordinarily made to the contemplative and mystical disposition of the beloved disciple. Such a reference is correct, for the contemplative viewpoint embraces the spiritual reality in a manner at once entire, spontaneous, and timeless.

[3] An important exception is found in the geographical and chronological annotations in John's Gospel. In this exception we may correctly see the added intention of supplementing the Synoptic account of Jesus' public life.

18

The task of a true historian is twofold: critical and synthetic. He must institute an inquiry into the true circumstances of the facts and then arrange this complex of acts and occurrences into a meaningful whole. This critical attitude is not present in John because he is the *witness* and the *beloved disciple*. This does not mean that he falsifies his material, but simply that it is not his intention to trace the causal connection between the various events or to arrange them in a meaningful order according to the human manner of judging them. In John's view everything in the world has its place through that particular disposition by which he sees everything in Christ. However, this is not history in the sense which we commonly attribute to the word.

As far as historicity in the strict sense—the truth of what is related—is concerned, the modern reader will do well to note that according to our standards St. John handles his material very freely. This is a point which must be stressed. A serious reader cannot simply ignore the principal aspect of the Johannine problem, which is concerned with the historicity of the fourth Gospel and its relationship to the Synoptics. Although this is not the proper place to treat the problem, nevertheless some observations on it must be made. Even Christian antiquity was aware that John subjects his material to his leading thoughts. This is what Clement of Alexandria had in mind when he called the Gospel of St. John "pneumatic," spiritual.[4]

For the Catholic who believes that divine inspiration excludes all error, this spiritual freedom has its limits. But the point is: where do these limitations lie in the concrete? It is extremely difficult to determine this, since we must not judge John according to our modern norms. Still, everything depends on a just evaluation of John's intention, since in Catholic teaching the sense which the writer intends is the one that is inspired by God.[5]

Thus, to put our finger on the chief difficulty: was it John's intention to repeat exactly the many words of Jesus which he records in his Gospel? Or may we suppose that because of his fixed purpose, because of his personal inclination and of the spirit of his Gospel, he casts these words in a form which is properly his own and not really that of Christ? May we even go so far as to suppose that he records as the words of Jesus things which were really only implied in the Master's words and which must thus in their final form be attributed to John rather than to Jesus? It is possible that the formulation of these questions may seem superfluous to the modern

[4] See Eusebius of Caesarea, *Hist. Eccl.,* VI, 14, 7.
[5] Occasional exceptions of the typical or figurative sense of Holy Scripture need not be considered here.

20

reader; but that there is reason for expressing them is evident from what follows. How must one explain the fact that the words of Jesus in St. John are so entirely unlike His words in the Synoptics? [6]

If one will compare a random speech of Jesus as recorded in the fourth Gospel with His words as found in the older Gospels, a great difference is immediately apparent. This does not mean that the Synoptics and John are contradictory or that they contain some irreconcilable opposition; but one feels that he is wandering in two realms of thought utterly heterogeneous. The atmosphere is unlike. To take a real example: where in John will you find the parables of the Synoptics or the pithy sayings of the Sermon on the Mount? The remark generally made concerning this difficulty, that in the Synoptics Jesus addresses the simple folk of Galilee, whereas in John His audience is composed of the intelligentsia of Jerusalem, the *Jews,* is only partially true and not pertinent. Even in the Synoptics we find accounts of disputes which Jesus had with the leaders of the capital city (e.g., Mt. 21:23—22:46); yet the contrast with the words of Jesus as recorded by St. John is striking. On the other hand, the renowned speech

---

[6] As is self-evident, these observations are true only in a general sense. An exception is found, for example, in the Johannine logion of Mt. 11:27 (Lk. 10:22).

21

at Capharnaum (Chap. 6), which was addressed primarily to the Galileans, is distinctly Johannine.

This brings us to another aspect of the problem. In the fourth Gospel, Jesus speaks in the same style as does the Baptist, and both speak in the style in which John writes the Gospel and the Epistle.[7] One thing is certain: one cannot seek the explanation of this phenomenon by assuming that John writes in the manner in which Jesus spoke, that because of long and loving contemplation the words of the Master and His manner of speaking became so much a part of the beloved disciple that he could not write otherwise. All competent scholars are agreed that the Synoptics more closely approximate the actual words of Jesus than does St. John. The style of Jesus' words was surely that of the Jewish rabbi, though it must be admitted that His axioms far surpass those of the Talmud both in spontaneity and in originality. This style is found faithfully in the Sermon on the Mount, for instance, but not in the fourth Gospel.

From all this only one conclusion may be drawn: John treated his material very freely, particularly the

[7] This must again be considered a generic assertion. There are indeed some differences: the characteristics of John's own manner of thinking and of writing are not so outstanding in the words of Jesus as they are elsewhere. Here we encounter the rather relative relationship of the writer to what may be called historical accuracy.

words of Jesus, and this to such an extent that we must perhaps say that we can no longer call them literal. He has faithfully preserved their substance, but they have been completely recast. One may compare it to an old theme that has been reworked; to some classic motif that has been adapted by a modern writer. The transposition may have the appearance of a new work, but an experienced ear will detect the original theme immediately. This is true in a higher sense of the way in which St. John transmits the words of Jesus. However, St. John intimates to his reader that he has done this, and that he has done it intentionally.

These observations on historicity concern principally the words of Jesus; only in a lesser degree do they apply to the narrative sections. One need only recall the emphasis with which St. John calls himself a witness. At the same time it is true that even many narrative sections are directly subordinated to his *leading ideas*. Thus the miracle of the healing of the man born blind is a *sign* of Christ as the Light; the resurrection of Lazarus is a graphic expression of the thought that Christ is Life and gives Life. The miracle of the multiplication of the loaves serves perhaps as the historical introduction to the speech in the synagogue of Capharnaum, but it can be viewed also as a prelude to the theme: The Bread of Life.

John does not narrate these miracles as mere proof of the truth of Jesus' mission. He is much more intent upon expressing his ideas in concrete form by choosing those facts which in the material order are a symbol of that spiritual reality which Christ is. This symbolism pervades his entire Gospel. It extends even to such details as the well known: "Now it was night" (13:30) in the account of Judas' betrayal. As a true spiritual writer, St. John seldom designates the hidden sense; he leaves the reader seek it. It is quite evident that these symbols may not be considered as pure literary fiction. It follows both from the goal which John had in mind and from his quality as *witness* that the truth of what is narrated must necessarily be supposed. Thus we see that the most *symbolic* accounts are at the same time also very realistic, particularly from a psychological point of view. The classic example of this convergence is the extremely vivid narrative of the healing of the man born blind (Chapter 9).

Thus we have finally come to a point from which we can form some idea of the special character of the fourth Gospel. It is not pure history, though it recounts historical facts. In spite of all its symbolism it is still very real. It is the work of a contemplative, but not of one who no longer could distinguish between the real and the ideal, as Loisy would have it. It is the work of a man who shows us that he not only contemplated the truth but that he was also privileged to see and to touch the Christ, the Word of Life. If one were permitted only one word to express the peculiar character of John's Gospel, the term "theological" would be most apt, as long as one does not understand it as do the students of scholastic or systematic theology, but in the sense of knowledge of God. This is what the Greek Church means when it calls John the "Theologian," the seer of God. It was necessary that the work of him who bore witness: "We have seen his glory," should have such a character. For he had seen the splendor of divinity which radiated from the countenance of Jesus, which emanated from His person. This was the light in which John saw the entire world. It is this luster of Christ, the Son of God, which will also enlighten our souls, if only we approach the Gospel of the beloved disciple with faith and reverence, with that disposition of soul which befits man when placed before divine revelation.

CHAPTER TWO

A Few Characteristic Ideas

I. Light

The three spheres—Christ, the Light—the light and the darkness—the man born blind —condemnation because of the rejection of the light—Christianity as the light.

NOTHING is more characteristic of St. John's way of thinking and, indeed, of his entire Gospel than his use of the term *light*. This is perhaps one of the points wherein we understand him least. He does not use the word with unreasonable frequency; [1] but he *always* uses it in very significant passages and *never* in the common, physical sense of the word.[2] If we classify the texts in which he uses

[1] 22 times in the Gospel and 6 times in the First Epistle.
[2] 11:9–10 is only an apparent exception.

this term, we may divide them into three categories: [3] those pertaining to God (I 1:5–7); those pertaining to Christ (1:4–5, 7–9; 3:19–21; 8:12; 9:5; 12:46); and those in which the term light is applied to man (1:4; 8:12; 12:35; I 1:7; 2:8–11). Yet this differentiation must not be made too strictly, for Christ is the Light of men. Such a combination is typical of St. John. Whereas our theology is constructed systematically in horizontal fashion with successive tracts on the existence of God, the Trinity, Creation, Christ the Redeemer, the Church, Grace, and so forth, St. John draws his line of thought vertically through the three spheres of God, Christ, and Christians. God is the Light, and the Logos is the Light of men, and the Christian is in the Light. Just as the Father has Life in Himself, so the Son is Life, and the Christian possesses this Life in faith. This ordering of ideas gives a strong cohesion to John's theological thought and draws the believer directly into the sphere of the divine life. On the other hand it also brings with it that interchangeableness of concepts which we have mentioned above.

The incarnate Logos is really the true Light. In St. John's way of looking at things it is self-evident that the Father is the fullness of Light, just as He

[3] Here we must make exception for 11:9–10 and for 5:35 where light is an ordinary metaphor for John the Baptist.

"has life in himself" (5:26). However he expresses this thought only once, and that in his Epistle (I 1:5–7), and even then adds immediately that he has received this revelation as a "message" from Christ and that it is a part, or better a summary, of the apostolic preaching. Christ is our divine light precisely because He is the revelation of the Father. The Apostle insists upon this constantly. "The Word was with God . . . in him was life, and the life was the light of men . . ." (1:1–4). This is the great event in history which St. John contemplates with respectful astonishment and loving gratitude: the plenitude of divine Life and Light has come forth from the bosom of the divinity (I 1:2 ff.) and has appeared among us in the person of Jesus Christ. Almost as great is the tremendous and incomprehensible tragedy of the world: "the world knew him not," for from the very beginning the darkness has been opposed to the Light (1:5 ff.). John rears his concept of the world on a great antithesis; his history is a drama. The darkness consists in the denial and overthrow of divine revelation. Just as the Light is the manifestation of the divine truth, so the darkness is a futile but terrible attempt to blot out the operation of the Light. The stage of this struggle is the spirit of man.

With painful bewilderment St. John observes

that the majority of men shun the Light. The world did not receive Him (1:5) and His own rejected Him (1:11). Men have loved the darkness rather than the Light (3:19). Although this terminology is generic, St. John has very specific things in mind, incidents of which he himself was a witness. He had himself seen and experienced the sorrowful act of the Jewish people rejecting its Messias. He had endured the first Roman persecutions of the Christians, and he was well aware that the world would never adopt a different attitude toward Christ (14:17; 15:18 ff.).

The marvelous radiance of the eternal divine Light in the person of Jesus, its soft glow on the man who humbly accepts this revelation, and its fiery brilliance which exposes the dullness of proud unbelief, are all graphically described in the account of Chapter 9 relating the healing of the man born blind. The light of the eye which Jesus grants to the afflicted man is a symbol, one might almost say a material exemplification, of that divine illumination which Jesus sheds upon the heart of the man who believes. This is indicated by the very name of the pool to which he is sent, the first his eyes had ever beheld; for the name *Siloe* means "Sent." And Jesus grants him the gift of faith, which is true sight. Jesus Himself said: "For judgment have I come into this world, that they who do not see may see, and they who see may become blind" (9:39). It is the Pharisees who are truly blind because they remain unbelieving, or, as Jesus puts it, they are blinded by the fierce brilliance of the Light which He is and which they refuse to accept. This is why He came into the world, to be a judgment, to be an irrevocable line of division (*krisis*), to be a sign of contradiction.

It is one of the characteristics of John's timeless view on things that he sees this judgment not only in the future (5:26–29) but as something which is taking place even now in the separation and distinction of the different spirits (3:19–21; 5:24; 9:39). It is in this earthly existence, fragile and perishable though it is, that the roots of an eternal life are planted. A man's destiny is determined here below by the attitude which he has toward the incarnate Word, the Light. The Apostle expresses this most clearly in a remark which he adds to the account of the Lord's discourse with Nicodemus: "Now this is the judgment: The light has come into the world, yet men have loved the darkness rather than the light, for their works were evil. For everyone who does evil hates the light, and does not come to the light, that his deeds may not be exposed. But he who does the truth comes to the light that his deeds may

31

be made manifest, for they have been performed in God" (3:19–21).

The judgment does not refer to some vague and distant future, it is taking place now. The masses exclude themselves from the Light: the Jews remain obstinate, the Gentiles persist in their spiritual blindness (cpr. Eph. 4:17–19; Rom. 1:18 ff.). They reject the light of Christianity by living immoral lives. Whoever behaves badly abhors the light of day. Similarly the man who lives an immoral life abhors the Light of Christ, which manifests the interior wickedness of his deeds. But he who lives *the truth* feels attracted by the Light, for his deeds are performed in God. In this passage the Light again finds its source and center in Christ. He is the Light and He brings Light into the world. This is a spiritual reality that has an active influence in the moral order. It is not merely a lovely glow, but a fiery brilliance which divides the spirits, compels men either to love or to hate, bares the moral nature of man to its core. As usual, John sees all these things in their ultimate consequences; he presents them as they are, without weakening them or obscuring them by fine nuances.

With Christ, the Light came into the world (12:46 and elsewhere); and when He returned to the Father, whom He had never left, the Light remained shining in the darkness through Christians who have within themselves His Spirit and the principle of divine life (I 3:9–24; 4:13). The Epistle speaks more clearly about the Light as the religious sphere-of-life of Christianity than does the Gospel (see I 1:5–7; 2:8–10). There the Christian mode of life is characterized as a "walking in the Light" which is God and is revealed in Christ and has also risen in us, "because the darkness has passed away and the true light is now shining." The infallible expression of this Light is found in Christian fraternal charity, in the fulfilling of that commandment which is simultaneously old and new. It is as old as Christianity, since it has its origin in God's eternal essence, Love. It is new, because it belongs to that new creation which Christ brought; and it is something which must always be exercised anew under all sorts of conditions and in all sorts of ways. Christian charity is something dynamic. It may never become static either in the Christian community or in the individual.

By thus analyzing the texts, the rich content of these complex representations of the Light slowly becomes apparent. The Light has its origin in God, it appears in Christ, it gleams in the Christian revelation, it is the beneficent glow of Christian life and love. Christ is the unifying element in this diversity.

33

In giving a definition of the Johannine concept of Light we might best offer this: The Light is Christ as the revelation of the divinity.[4]

[4] It is precisely this specifically Christian character, its relationship to the historical person of Christ, which distinguishes John's representation of light from all forms of Gnosticism. In the Gnostic doctrine Light is looked upon as something almost physical, as the sphere, the habitation, or the materialization of the principle of good (e.g., among the Mandeans); or in a more philosophical sense as being identical with the faculty of thinking and with the divine spirit (*Corpus Hermeticum*), but always in opposition to "darkness" which is ultimately limited by or identified with matter. It is clear that the Gnostic antithesis of spirit and matter is not to be found in John. "The Word was made flesh." Christianity, even the Christianity of John, with its Incarnation (1:14), Eucharist (6:48f. and also 6:64), resurrection of bodies (5:28–29) is not a gradual liberation from matter, but from sin; and sin, which is apostasy from God par excellence, constitutes in John's way of thinking a rejection of the Light, an obstinate refusal to believe in Christ. On the other hand, it cannot be maintained that the Johannine use of the term light differs in no essential point from the diction of the rest of the New Testament. The absolute aspect of such expressions as "God is Light" and "I have come a light into the world" (12:46) have no parallel in the Bible and may have been formally influenced by Gnosticism.

II. Life

Life in God, in Christ, and in man—the supernatural character of life—eternal life here on earth—Johannine vitalism.

THE notion of life occupies the central position in John's theology. "And this is the testimony, that God has given us eternal life, and this life is in his Son" (I 5:11). This is the essence of the message of salvation as presented by John: Christ, the Son of God, is the source of life for mankind. The imperishable gift of Christian salvation is *life*.

As we analyze the texts in which John treats of life, we see that the three divisions which were made when we spoke about *light* also apply here. Relatively few texts speak about the life which is *in God, in the Father;* [5] yet this particular aspect is presupposed as the source from which everything else flows. The first two texts are of special importance. The Father "has life in himself"; it is absolutely His own, independent of all else. The Father is also the "living" one. He is the beginning without beginning (*principium sine principio*). The Apostle speaks more frequently about the Son and His life. The incarnate Word is for mankind the unique and

[5] See 5:26; 6:58; 12:50; 15:20(?).

35

unfathomable fountain of life, a veritable spring from which life pours forth. There is scarcely a text in which the life of Christ is not in some manner associated with mankind. John's whole teaching on the life of the Son is marvelously contained in I 1:2: "And the Life was made known and we have seen, and now testify and announce to you, the Life Eternal which was with the Father, and has appeared to us." The Logos is the Life Eternal. Without distinction, John says both that Christ is the life,[6] and that life is in Him.[7] Christ's life is "with the Father." He possesses life as independently as does the Father; His life is also a source of life for others, yet He receives it from the Father.[8] For He is the Son, who has all things from the Father (*principium principiatum*). Furthermore, this life "was made known" to us; this is the historic saving mission of Christ, the reason why He became man.[9] Thirdly and lastly, there is the consideration of life in man. John presents this last concept concisely in 17:3: "Now this is everlasting life, that they may know thee, the only true God, and him whom thou hast sent, Jesus Christ." He proceeds to clarify this complex statement gradually by means of other illustrations. For

[6] 11:25; 14:6; 15:20 (?).
[7] 1:4; 15:11.
[8] 5:26; 6:27.
[9] 1:4; 10:10,28; 17:2; I 5:11–12.

36

man, to possess life is to be saved from the wrath of God, to escape judgment, perdition, death (3:15, 16,36; 5:24). Man attains this life by *faith* in Christ, by believing that He is the Son and the One sent by the Father,[10] by hearing His word (5:24), by coming to Him (5:40) by beholding the Son (6:40), by following Him (8:12). Thus faith, understood in the full Johannine sense as *complete surrender of one's personality,* is the one great means of receiving life.[11] This inner life is nourished with "the bread of life" (chapter 6); its proof of authenticity is the continuous exercise of fraternal charity (I 3:14–15); it will reach its full development in the glorious "resurrection of life" (5:29; 6:40, 54; 11:26). It is the Spirit of the Father and the Son which in a mysterious manner becomes in the heart of every believer an ever-flowing fountain of life (4:10–11,14; 7:38).

It is evident even from so brief a summation that we are facing here the central theme of John's message. Here, too, it is important to understand well the simplicity of his language. John never uses the term "life" in a neutral sense, with a purely philosophical, cosmic, or naturalistic signification. By life,

---

[10] 3:15–16,35; 5:24,39,40; 6:40,47; 11:26; 20:31; I 5:13.

[11] It is evident that such a faith includes the acceptance of the whole economy of salvation and the reception of the sacraments; see 3:3ff.

as by light, he always intends a deep religious meaning, or better, a deep Christian and divine meaning. The Christian life, which the believer possesses because of his union with the Son, is of the same kind as that which the Father has "in himself." This life is the only one worthy of the name, for it is a participation in the plenitude of the divine being and activity. This unworldly character, far removed from all that is profane, is also apparent from the only epithet which John ever applies to it: "eternal." *Life* and *eternal life* are used indiscriminately and have an identical meaning. It is qualified only in view of the divine immensity. Through Christ man shares in this divine gift, which is nothing less than a communion with the Father and the Son. This communion is already begun here on earth through faith in the Christian revelation.

The point that strikes us most in the fourth Gospel is the paradox of the believer already possessing *eternal life* while still on this earth—even before death.[12] At times it would almost seem that heaven can add nothing more to this beatitude, one beyond the realm and influence of time. In the New Testament the death of the Christian is never looked upon as a defeat; for St. John it is only a transition. When Jesus speaks of His imminent death John

[12] 5:24; 11:25; I 3:14ff.

calls it a passing out of this world to the Father (13:1). Jesus deliberately lays down His natural principle of life, the *psychē* (10:17–18); but life itself He cannot lose, for He *is* life. So also this life in the Christian is of itself unlimited and imperishable, "eternal." [13] "Amen, amen, I say to you, if anyone keep my word, he will never see death" (8:50). "He who believes in me, even if he die, shall live; and whoever lives and believes in me, shall never die" (11:25–26). What people ordinarily call "dying" does not have this signification for the Christian. Death has been reduced to a meaningless incident. John has pondered this important concept so deeply and penetrated it so keenly that it would sometimes seem as though there is no longer any need of the Judgment or of the second coming of Christ (3:18–19; 5:24). This, however, is only an apparent conclusion. The Apostle remains in perfect accord with the earliest Christian tradition. He is fully aware that we do not possess eternal life perfectly here and now. He does not remove all distinction between grace and glory: ". . . it has not yet appeared what we shall be. We know that, when he appears, we shall be like to him, for we shall see him just as he is" (I 3:2).[14]

[13] In this manner we can understand at least to some extent the remarkable assertion of I 3:6–9 that "Whoever is born of God does not commit sin."

[14] See also 5:25ff.; I 2:28; 4:17.

The place which the Kingdom of Heaven occupies in the teaching of the Synoptics is assigned to life in St. John's Gospel. Both are that precious pearl, to obtain which the believer will give up everything else. Still, there is a certain difference in viewpoint. John's Christendom is more intimate, more profound; it is a more personal possession, a fuller consciousness of the divine Principle. But it is not a passive possession, something which is obtained and preserved in bourgeois fashion. On the other hand, we do not find in St. John the fierce impetuosity of Paul's wrestling: "Not that I have already obtained this, or already have been made perfect, but I press on hoping that I may lay hold of that for which Christ Jesus has laid hold of me" (Phil. 3:12). At the time when the aged John wrote his Gospel, his spirit had been deeply and firmly rooted in the contemplation of imperishable values and eternal truths. Nevertheless, for him too, life is a risk, an adventure: "He who loves his life (*psychē*), loses it; and he who hates his life (*psychē*) in this world, keeps it unto life (*zōē*) everlasting" (12:25). This audacity does not spring from a carelessness about life, but from a faith which assures him of a higher life. For John life is not some intractable, spontaneous outburst of vital powers; rather it is the germination of a divine "seed" (I 3:9), and comes into being

40

through a birth from God (1:13). It is absolutely independent of the influence of biological forces (1:13); reason itself has no power over it. The insufficiency of the human spirit placed face to face with the divine revelation is nowhere so apparent as in the fourth Gospel, where the words of Jesus always meet with misunderstanding, where it is just the *leaders* of the people who remain blind to the divine Light. Life is God's great gift in and through Christ, given to him who believes, to the spirit which submits itself, to the heart which abandons itself entirely to Him who is the Way, the Truth, and the Life.

III. Love

Eros and agapē—"God is Love"—God's love in Christ and in man—the dynamic and operative character of Johannine love—love, joy, peace.

TO THE ancient world, Christendom revealed itself as love—and Christians of all ages must remain lovers or cease to be Christians. In Greek, the international language at the time of the Apostles, this Christian love was called *agapē*. This was a word with which the Greeks were not acquainted in

41

its substantive form, though they used the verbal form from which the substantive is derived.[15] They used the word *eros* to express their type of love. But the *agapē* overcame the *eros*. Shortly after the death of St. John, Ignatius the Martyr wrote: "My *eros* has been crucified. There no longer exists within me that fire, which is attracted to and loves matter, but there exists within me that living water which says: 'Come to the Father.' "[16]

Eros signifies passionate love, that elementary ardor, that joy in the good things of life, that appetite of the flesh, that impetuous desire, that invincible god which triumphs over everything. No one has ever praised *eros* as did Plato in the *Symposium*. In his view, love is basically the desire for corporal beauty, but this is not its final objective. It rises from the body to the spirit, and from the spirit to "divine beauty" itself, to the eternal ideas. By this admirable dialectic Plato attempts to avoid the excessively corporal and passionate elements which are inherent in the *eros*. One may be assured that this exalted notion of *eros,* as an idea, remained an exception, and that in practice it wielded no influence on Greek and Hellenistic love life. But even

[15] At any rate it was not in common usage. There are perhaps only one or two places where the word may be found in pre-Christian profane texts.

[16] *Ad Rom.* 7,2.

were we to accept the *eros* as it is depicted in the *Symposium* of Plato and to judge it in its most ideal form, we would still be struck by the fact that this concept of love is purely naturalistic. It could not be otherwise. Its basis and starting point are the passions. It is only after continual purification, and by following a narrow and difficult path of which only a few initiates are capable that man finally arrives at more spiritual objects. The Platonic *eros* is developed on ascending lines. It is thus Plato describes the development of the human spirit, its slow gaining of consciousness, its laborious progress toward the knowledge and the love of the world of divine ideas.

The Christian *agapē,* on the other hand, is not the fruit of a gradual development or the result of a spiritual progress. It is not a purified passion. It comes from God and is His gift (I 4:7). It does not ascend from some human principle, but descends from the bosom of God only to return again. This love is not reserved to a few philosophical initiates and unavailable to the masses who are incapable of knowing or of judging these matters; it is destined for all and must envelop all. Neither the body nor material things play an important role in the *agapē* (except as an element of sacrifice), though it is ready to bend compassionately over the corporal needs of the lowliest slave. It does not lead to abstract philosophical contemplation, but to simple and continual action. It is free from passion and instinct; for this child of God, too, is born "not of blood, nor of the will of flesh, nor of the will of man." It has all the strength and the will-to-action which characterized the love of the Old Testament without being bound by its jealous exclusiveness. Like the Hellenistic *eros,* it is cosmopolitan and universal; it is not restricted by boundaries either of state or of race. But it is vibrant with a purity and strong with an unshaken fidelity, unknown to the *eros.*

By centering his *agapē* in God—and this is worth repeating—by fixing it in the Father who has revealed Himself through Christ, St. John has exceeded both the narrowness of the Jew who loved only his fellow countryman, and the *eros* of the Greek which had lost in stability and purity what it had gained in universality. It is in St. John that we have that admirable phrase, which has had no precedent and will never be surpassed: "God is love" (I 4:7–8,16). God is not an impersonal principle of all things, an immanent world-spirit; nor is He the unmoved mover, an exalted idea, a personified natural force, a Homeric superman, a blind and hard fate. He is not even that unique and transcendent Majesty, the "Holy of Israel" of Judaism (though it

44

must be honestly admitted that the Johannine formula did find an anticipation in the Old Testament.
One need only think of the loving Father and the
tenderly loving Bridegroom of the Prophets). He is
the immeasurable and personal Goodness which
shares its being first of all with the Logos, who is
"with the Father," and then, through the Logos, with
the entire world. "For God so loved the world that
he gave his only-begotten Son . . ." (3:16). If the
essence of God is love, and if Christ is the supreme
revelation of God, *the Incarnate God,* then He must
also be the supreme revelation, the highest realization of God's love. This is precisely what St. John
teaches (I 4:9–10,16). Jesus is the incarnate love of
God, especially in His death, whereby *He has saved
the world,* that is, man, who so needed salvation. His
blood cleanses us (I 1:7), "he is a propitiation for
our sins, not for ours only but also for those of the
whole world" (2:2).

Thus Jesus is the Mediator of divine love. This
love is entirely focused upon the Son and through
Him it reaches men (17:23 ff.; 14:21 ff.). The *agapē*
does not lose its peculiar nature in man. It remains
in the believer a divine energy ever tending toward
a sharing of itself, toward action, toward unity, toward the completion of the divine circle: Father—
Son—believer. This is why St. John so strongly em-

phasizes fraternal charity. It is through fraternal charity that even here on earth the divine association has its origin. This divine communion is not of this world, but it is a copy, or better, a realization of that heavenly union of love which exists between the Father and the Son. "That all may be one, even as thou, Father, in me and I in thee; that they also may be one in us, that the world may believe that thou hast sent me. . . . that they may be perfected in unity, and that the world may know that thou hast sent me, and that thou hast loved them even as thou hast loved me" (17:21,23). Jesus' entire work of salvation is directed to this one end: that the believers may share in that love which is the essence of God, "And I have made known to them thy name, and will make it known, *in order that the love with which thou hast loved me may be in them, and I in them*" (17:26).[17]

We must not suppose that Johannine love is an abstract and unreal notion, something which may be pleasing to some contemplative soul, but which has no application to the real situations of everyday life. Although this *agapē* is not a blind biological force, it possesses nonetheless all the captivating ardor and all the powerful impulses of the *eros*. St. John knows

[17] Later we shall speak of love as the "rule of life" of Christianity, as *the* great obligation of Christians.

the force of love. The ordinary representation of the Apostle as a timid young man is entirely false. Leaving aside the fact that his writings betray a violent temperament, an ardent, almost a fanatical nature (one need think only of the Apocalypse), even the few historical data that we have concerning him contradict the customary portrayals. There is nothing sentimental about the "son of thunder" who is ready to call fire from heaven on the inhospitable Samaritans (Mk. 3:17; Lk. 9:54). His love is a vital energy. "He who does not love abides in death" (I 3:14) . . . "And everyone who loves is born of God, and knows God" (I 4:7). This sounds almost like a metaphysical analysis of love. There can be no doubt that John is thinking here primarily of Christian love; whoever does not love God or his brother remains in everlasting death. However, he has a special reason for twice expressing himself in vague and general terms. He knows that what he has written is an unchangeable truth, that whoever does not love abides in death. Only love can release the latent forces of the soul. It is love which awakens in the soul of every man unlimited powers either for good or for evil. Love can transform a man in an amazing way. John knows this. He has experienced it within himself, and has seen in others how the love of God in Christ has aroused all energies and led to the habitual practice of Christian charity.

This realism in St. John's notion of love is noteworthy. For him, this love does not depend on one's feelings; it has nothing in common with sentimentalism or with a vague humanitarianism. The concrete object of its activity is one's *fellow man,* whom it considers as a *brother.* Action alone proves its genuineness. This criterion recurs constantly in the writing of the Apostle and is applied equally to the love of God (14:15,21 ff.) and to love of fellow men: "My dear children, let us not love in word, neither with the tongue, but in deed and in truth" (I 3:18). It would almost seem that the love of God must give place to the love of fellow men, since this latter is more tangible, more easily attainable, less subject to illusions: "If anyone says, 'I love God,' and hates his brother, he is a liar. For how can he who does not love his brother, whom he sees, love God, whom he does not see? And this commandment we have from him, that he who loves God should love his brother also" (I 4:20–21). The *agapē* does not recoil at the supreme sacrifice: "In this we have come to know his love, that he laid down his life for us; and we likewise ought to lay down our life for the brethren" (I 3:16).

The Apostle truly believed in love (I 4:16). Christian love has nothing of that sickly sentimentalism which kills joy and has its origin in a fear of life: "Perfect love casts out fear" (I 4:18). It casts out even the fear of the annihilating judgment of God; how much more so the terrors of human existence. On the contrary, love is the power which embraces life in its totality and renders it immeasurably fruitful. All its inclinations are positive. It is not the voluptuousness of the immature, who do not *dare* to live, as Nietzsche supposes. Joy is her inseparable companion: "Abide in my love. If you keep my commandments you will abide in my love, as I also have kept my Father's commandments, and abide in his love. These things I have spoken to you that my joy may be in you, and that your joy may be made full" (15:10–11). The joy of loving and of knowing that one is loved is enduring happiness, which not even the world can take from our poor heart, for "God is greater than our heart and knows all things" (I 3:20). This is the peace which Christ has left us: "Peace I leave with you, my peace I give to you. . . ." (14:27).

CHAPTER THREE

Christ, the Focal Point of the Fourth Gospel

❖❖❖❖❖❖❖❖❖

I. A General View

The extent of John's preoccupation with Christ—his Gospel is entirely fixed on the person of Christ—difference between John's mode of expression and ours—the manner in which Jesus revealed Himself to His contemporaries—the extremely human portrait of Christ in the fourth Gospel—the superhuman background.

THE extent to which the personality of Christ dominated John's thought becomes apparent even in a cursory reading of his Gospel. A more profound study of St. John's writings will reveal how completely he is filled with Jesus. It would almost seem that the spirit of the beloved disciple can see creation only in and through the Master, in a manner analogous to that wherein Jesus' own consciousness—in the words of the fourth Gospel—is filled completely with the Father. We are forcefully reminded here of Jesus' words: ". . . that they may be one, even as we are one: I in them and thou in me" (17:22–23). For St. John, Jesus is a continuous and operative presence, an atmosphere of life and love in which his own soul is completely immersed. John is really "in Christ," he "remains in him," he "lives through him." Christ has revealed Himself to the Apostle and has made His abode with him (14:21,23). This union through grace in the depth of his soul has become conscious and almost transparent to John. Christ is always present in his consciousness, even when he is not speaking expressly about the Master. There is a small peculiarity of style in his writing—negligible in itself, but all the more significant because of its unobtrusiveness— which reveals this constant spiritual presence. Often in his First Epistle John speaks of Christ without mentioning Him by name. Without further introduction he abruptly uses the pronoun "he," for instance, in that admirable passage: "In this we have come to know his love, that *he* laid down his life for us" (I 3:16). His readers know well who is meant: it is He who has filled John's spirit and utterly dominates his life.

Jesus is the central point of John's view on the world. His adorable and always vivid personality has broken the rigidity of expression and formula which might otherwise have easily led to some system of Gnosticism. Such concepts as *light, life, love, truth,* obtain their full content and meaning only through Jesus of Nazareth. His appearance on this earth was the decisive moment of history; with His coming a new age has begun. "The true light is now shining" (I 2:8), "for the Law was given through Moses; [but] grace and truth came through Jesus Christ" (1:17). St. John evaluates all things in the light of Christ. He knows God only through Him, for "no one has at any time seen God, but the only-begotten Son . . . has revealed him" (1:18). Mankind is divided into two classes: those who believe in the light and, like the Son, are born of God; and those who reject Him. It is also worthy of note that the Apostle never calls himself by name, but refers to himself in relation to Jesus as "the disciple whom Jesus loved."

It goes without saying that in all the Gospels Jesus is the central personality; but the fourth Gospel far exceeds the others in stressing this focalization. The discourses which are preserved by John have no content other than Jesus. This is true in a sense of the other Gospels also, for the Kingdom of God, of which they treat, was inaugurated by Christ. In the beautiful words of Origen, Christ Himself is that Kingdom. But the idea is much more pointed in St. John. As proof, one need only compare the Sermon on the Mount with the Farewell Address. Christ Himself is also the subject matter of the great polemic discourses as they are summarized by St. John in 5:19–47; 8:12–59; for in them Jesus manifests and defends His personality, His relationship to the Father, His origin, and His mission. He describes Himself as the Light of the World, the Bread of Life, the Good Shepherd. This is entirely in accord with John's purpose.

We must be mindful, however, that to express this fruitful contemplation of Christ St. John uses expressions and formulas which differ from ours. For centuries we have been accustomed to the clear-cut formulas of the great dogma of Jesus as a divine person existing in a twofold nature—divine and human. This precise formula only came into being in the course of ages after much theological thought and dispute. It presupposes certain philosophical concepts, such as nature and person, and is manifestly the fruit of theological reflection. Hence we must not think it strange if we do not find these formulas in the New Testament, not even in St. John. Nor may we conclude that, because these formulas are not expressed as such in the sacred books of the New Testament, the *substance* of the dogma is not contained there. On the contrary, it was these very writings, and especially the Gospel of St. John, which supplied the scriptural foundation for this Christological dogma. Nonetheless, it remains a fact that the writers of the New Testament, including St. John who wrote last of all and has won for himself the special title of theologian, did not experience this theological development. It is consequently not right for us to interpret their sayings (as well as those of Jesus, who always accommodated Himself to the intelligence of His audience) *directly* according to the concepts of our own scientific theology. There is great danger of adding something foreign to the thought of St. John if we constantly and persistently ask ourselves: Does Jesus here speak as man or as God?

For the writers of the New Testament, Jesus was undoubtedly both true man and true God—for He is the only Son of the Father—but they were not wont to make an explicit distinction between the divine and the human nature or between these natures and the divine person. For that matter, Jesus Himself did not make these distinctions either.[1] Had He used such terminology He would have been as unintelligible to His contemporaries as a man speaking about the telephone or the radio in the time of Copernicus. It is a mistake to seek in the Bible the whole body of Christian Dogma in its complete formulation. One may not forget that the term "bible" means *book,* and consequently a complex of ideas that have been crystallized into written form at a determined moment of time. Any book traces its origin to a certain people characterized by a peculiar mode of thought and expression; it is the work of a writer with a definite goal in mind. Any piece of writing is necessarily fixed, unchangeable, and historically limited. In this we find a great and an essential difference in the living teaching authority of the Church of Christ. Though faithful to and entirely dependent on revealed truth, this ecclesiastical teaching authority grows with humanity; it speaks the language of all times, because it is destined for all time; and it is intelligible to all. That is why it was to the Church that Christ entrusted His sacred books, and that is why He refers the faithful to the teaching authority of the Church: "Whoever hears you, hears me." He did not command His followers to

[1] Though at times He did suggest such a distinction; for example, see Mt. 22:41–45.

56

read and to examine; He told them to hear and to obey.

In like manner, the Gospel of St. John is necessarily limited in its spiritual horizon, so different from our own. One is not justified in saying that the difference between John and the Synoptics is that the latter view Jesus as man whereas John contemplates Him primarily as God. This statement does contain an element of truth, but it is based too much on the explicit distinction between the divine and the human nature—which we make so glibly—to be absolutely correct. For the Apostles and for their contemporaries in general, Jesus was primarily a specific historic and human figure. This man revealed Himself to them as the Son of God, united intimately with God in a way no man before Him had ever dared consider possible, no matter how great his holiness or how sublime his vocation. This consciousness of His own dignity, this incredible claim to divinity was supported by striking miracles, "signs" as St. John calls them, by superhuman goodness and moral power, by an exalted teaching which had wondrous drawing power. But Jesus never asserted that He was God in so many words. Such an affirmation could never have found acceptance among the Jews, bound as they were by their strict monotheism.

It is characteristic of divine mercy that it adapts itself to human weakness; thus Jesus revealed the mystery of His person only gradually. This process of progressive revelation is still discernible in substance in the simple narration of the Synoptics. Jesus adapted His preaching to the ideals existing at that time, to the expectation of the Kingdom of God and to the messianic hope. First He endeavored to purify the Jewish notion of the Kingdom of God. At the same time He tried to win over the hearts of men by His goodness and by His power of miracles and thus to make them receptive to His teaching. When the large majority of the Jews, however, persisted in clinging to their earthly and nationalistic ideals, Jesus more or less withdrew into the intimate circle of His friends, His *disciples*. To them He clarified the relationship that existed between the Kingdom of God and Himself. To them He revealed Himself as the Messias of the prophets, as the Son of Man, as the suffering Servant of Jahweh. To them He also revealed the intimate mystery of His personality, His divine Sonship. And then the small and timorous group of disciples was struck by the catastrophe of Jerusalem, by the scandal of the cross.

The Risen Savior found His little flock abashed and in great consternation. But there descended upon them the Spirit of Christ, the Spirit of truth, who led them to the fullness of truth and gave them understanding of all the things Jesus had taught: the significance of His mission, of His death and glorification, of His divine-human existence (14:26; 16:13). Then there began the conquest of the world for Christ, and together with this the period of the inner working of the Spirit, the period of faith and preaching, of *reflection* on Jesus, the era of the defense of the Christian teaching, of the refutation of heresies, and of theological reflection. In this living stream of Christian belief and thought the synoptic Gospels represent an older and less developed stage than does the fourth Gospel. Generally speaking they are dependent on the apostolic preaching of the faith, on the primitive catechesis. Later, John gives his own strongly personal view. This does not mean that he falsified the historical reality, but that from the vantage point of later development he saw things more in their essential and unchangeable form, and less in their transitory and changeable aspects. It is not to be wondered at therefore that in him we find few traces, if any, of that progression in Jesus' self-revelation as we see it in the Synoptics. From the first words of his Gospel he presents Jesus as the Logos, as the Only-begotten. The penetrating vision of his faith pierces all external appearances.

The result is that in the fourth Gospel Christ seems to be moving on a double plane, as though He were living in two worlds, but at home in only one of them. This dualism is expressed in substance in the short phrase of the Prologue: "The Word was made flesh." He is the Word, and He remains such. In this sense there can be no question of development or of change. But He became flesh in time, a true man of flesh and blood. This is the theme of St. John's Gospel. Unbelievers have often tried to present the Christ of St. John as an abstraction, as though He were not a real man, but an unreal shadow hovering above time and space, a "Christ of faith." This notion is based on a very one-sided interpretation of certain data in the fourth Gospel. One might be rather justified in maintaining that the picture which St. John has drawn of Jesus is more heartfelt and more human than that of the Synoptics. How perfectly natural and absolutely human are such scenes as that of Jesus speaking with the Samaritan woman, while "wearied as he was from the journey, he was sitting at the well" (4:6). Likewise the scene of the resurrection of Lazarus, the intense emotion which He can no longer restrain when He sees the sorrow of the others as He approaches the grave of His beloved friend: "See, how he loved him" (11:33–38). John alone has preserved for posterity the tragic tableau of the *"Ecce Homo"* (19:5) and that pitiful cry of the Crucified: "I thirst" (19:28). Notice the psychological finesse and delicate reserve in the triple questioning of Peter: "Do you love me" (21:15 ff.), or in that one word addressed to the grief-stricken Magdalene when He calls her by name and thus stirs her love: "Mary— Rabboni" (20:14 ff.). How human is that anguish which burdens His heart at the Last Supper and restrains Him from pouring forth His soul in intimate expressions of farewell as long as the traitor is present (13:1–31). How moving is that predilection which Jesus manifests for the "disciple whom he loved." Such details have not been written in order to give the heavenly and divine Logos a sort of human background. They are taken from life, from the memories of John's youth, conserved tenderly, and committed to writing in his old age. Thanks to them, there rises before our eyes even today the beautiful human picture of his divine friend.

Yet, more than anything else, this man is the Logos, the Son of God, whose divine and supernatural essence pervades His humanity. Perhaps we may formulate it as follows. We are accustomed to distinguishing clearly between the human and the divine in Jesus. But John sees Christ as a unity, as a totality. He sees the human as permeated and transfigured by the divine, as a revelation of God. The divine radiance, the *glory* of God shines through Him, and whoever has seen this glory and has believed may give testimony of it. This is the meaning of those pregnant words: "The Word was made flesh, and dwelt among us. And we saw his glory—glory as of the only-begotten of the Father—full of grace and of truth" (1:14). The consciousness of this man who is called Jesus is not a merely human consciousness.[2] It is supernatural: He is "not of this world" (8:23); it is independent of time: "before Abraham came to be, I am" (8:58). His time and His manner of reckoning time are different from those of this world; they are not determined by the circumstances and calculations of man. He does not live by earthly food, but by the will of His Father. In spite of all appearances, His death is not a hopeless failure, but a free surrender of His life because of love. His divine power is manifest even in the last moments of His life (18:6). In St. John's view, the death on the cross is no longer a scandal, but a "lifting up from the earth," the actual beginning of glory. This man, who hangs there alone, the apparent victim of the intrigues of those who are in authority, is in reality beyond the reach of all human and diabolic designs:

[2] This will be explained in greater detail later. For the moment it is sufficient to sketch a general picture of Jesus' personality, as John sees it.

"the prince of the world . . . has nothing in me" (14:30). If He humbles Himself to the very earth before His disciples, He does so with the full consciousness of His divine power and origin (13:3). He knows full well whence He came and whither He is going.

It is not a human story that opens the Gospel of St. John, but the mysterious and exalted song of a divine generation; and as it ends there arises before our astonished eyes the figure of the Risen Savior bearing the marks of His suffering, the Lamb which has been slain for the sins of the world. And we? We are left with only that one word, which St. Thomas spoke in behalf of us all: "My Lord and my God!" (20:28).[3]

[3] This is the real end of the Gospel, the final chord. What follows on this is a double epilogue (20:30–31 and all of chapter 21).

II. The Logos

The Prologue—Logos, the name of the pre-existing Christ—the Greek notion of logos—the Stoics—Philo—St. John's independence of his Hellenistic predecessors—the divine creative word in the Old Testament—Wisdom—Christ, the subject of primitive Christian preaching—Christ, the Word of God.

THE Prologue of St. John (1:1–18), the greater part of which (vv. 1–14) is ordinarily read as the last Gospel of the Mass, is in every respect the most exalted, and the most Johannine passage of the fourth Gospel. From time immemorial it has inspired admiration in its readers.[4] The opening verses, full of mystery and moving in admirable rhythm, are the climax of that monotonous majesty which characterizes the style of St. John. The Prologue is not a foreword in our sense of the term, nor is it a summary of the Gospel, although it does contain many of the ideas which we have already considered, such as life, light, darkness, faith, the world. It precedes the Gospel because it is principally concerned with the pre-existence, the pre-human existence of Christ.

[4] Even more so in its hearers; it is really meant to be recited.

64

This pre-existence of the Son of God and His transition (if one may use the term here) to a human, historic existence through the Incarnation form the principal theme of the Prologue. Significant and worthy of note is the special name which John applies to Christ only in the Prologue and does not use again in the entire Gospel—the name of Logos.[5] He abandons this name within the Prologue itself at the moment of the Incarnation in order to make room for the more generally accepted titles of the Redeemer: "And the *Word* was made flesh, and dwelt among us. And we saw his glory—glory as of the only-begotten of the Father—full of grace and of truth." The term "only-begotten" (*monogenes*) is also a strictly Johannine designation of Christ, but one that is directly intelligible. Only a few verses further on he begins to use the customary compounded proper name "Jesus Christ" (1:17). There is then no doubt that when St. John uses the name Logos he means the person of Jesus, of whose life and activity he was the fortunate witness. But his purpose in applying this name to Jesus in the Prologue and the idea he wishes to convey by using it are not so directly apparent.

The statements of St. John concerning the Logos

[5] It is used in reference to Christ also in I 1:1: "of the Word of Life"; but its use here is more vague, less personal than in the Gospel. See also Apoc. 19:13.

may be summarized as follows: the Logos exists from all eternity; He is with God from all eternity; He is God. An absolutely universal causality in the creation of things is attributable to Him 1:3.[6] Lastly, this Logos became man; or, in the marvelous realism of St. John's own words: "The Word was made flesh." As the Epistle puts it, He "was made known," He "has appeared to us." And with that the term Logos as a proper name disappears from the Gospel. One may thus conclude that St. John intends "Logos" to indicate the pre-human existence of Christ, the eternal background of His appearance in time on this earth. Jesus Himself describes this existence as being with the Father "before the world existed" (17:5). The Logos is distinguished from God because He is "with God"; yet at the same time He is God. These simple words express in an unequivocal manner that truth which theology later formulated as: The Logos is distinguished from the Father as person, but He possesses the same unique and in-

[6] The Greek word, *dia,* which is translated by *through* (see the Confraternity of Christian Doctrine text) frequently signifies instrumental causality. Since, in John's view, the Logos is truly God, there can be no question of a real dependence on the Father as the first or prime cause. Later theological reflection on the Father-Son relationship in the Trinity sees here expressed the idea that Jesus as the Son receives His creative activity as well as His very being from the Father, who is the Principle without beginning, though this happens without the bearing of dependency which characterizes the relationship of creatures toward God.

divisible divine nature. Thus in his Prologue St. John merely states more clearly what other early Christian writers had already said. For examples, one need only consult St. Paul, Rom. 1:4; 8:3; I Cor. 10:3 f.; Col. 1:16; Phil. 2:5 ff.

The term *logos* is something new. The Greek term signifies "word." The Latin Vulgate translates it in this manner, as do many of our modern languages such as German, Dutch, English. Nonetheless, the term "word" as it is used in modern languages is not entirely synonymous with the meaning of the original Greek. The Greek *logos* signifies not only the spoken word but also the interior word of the mind, the thought, the idea. Even the faculty of reasoning, the mind itself, can be designated by this word. Furthermore, because of the harmonious concept which the Greeks had of the universe, the objective order of things coincides with the subjective view of them; or better, man's reason discovers the regularity and the order of the cosmos. Thus the notion of logos also acquires a strongly objective character, and signifies the harmony and the inner coherence of the world to which the human logos corresponds, the world-order as it exists in man's consciousness.

The philosophy of the Stoics especially, which was very influential in Hellenistic times, adopted this notion of the logos and expanded it in a pantheistic sense. For the Stoics, the logos is the regulating principle immanent in the world; it evolves within the world and is nothing else but God Himself. Through his reason man shares in the divinity. And thus the divinity is immanent in man. Religion is the development of one's own human nature. "To obey God means to follow one's reason (logos)" was an axiom of the Stoics.

The notion of logos occupies a particularly important place in the works of the Alexandrian Jew, Philo. This man was a contemporary of Christ. It was his desire to harmonize the Jewish religion and the Old Testament with the Greek philosophy and culture of his time. One of the means by which he hoped to bring about this impossible synthesis was by exploiting the notion of the logos, so dear to the Greeks. For Philo, the logos was no longer merely an idea properly speaking, but a kind of personification, a mythological figure somewhere between an infinitely remote God and the world. Among his many logos-figures, only the divine logos is worthy of note here. This logos is not identical with God, as it was for the Stoics, but is a creature of God, an instrument of God. There are also passages in which it is called God, but then only in a secondary manner, as a God of lower rank. It is the image of God, the prototype of creation, a mediator between God and man, the high priest and intercessor for man before God. This logos plays an important role in Philo's view of creation.

It is readily understandable that the Prologue of the fourth Gospel is frequently compared with the various Hellenistic ideas of the logos, especially with that of Philo. Supposing that such a relationship between them does exist, one might consider it in one of two ways: either St. John is dependent on these others, so that they exercise a direct influence on his thought; or he is leading a polemic reaction against their ideology and is thus attributing to the term logos an essentially different signification, one fitting only when applied to the historic personality of Jesus of Nazareth. In the latter case there would be question only of a certain adaptation to the Greek spirit by the choice of the word logos.

If one peruses the writings of St. John with attention to the true sense, it becomes evident that he is not dependent on those Hellenistic speculations on the logos which were rife at his time. His Logos is an historic figure, the living person of Jesus, who was born in time, whom the Apostle "saw and handled," who died and rose again. Jesus is not merely an idea. Nor is He the immanent world-principle of the Stoics. He is not of this world, but He was sent into this world by the Father in order to save it. Nor may one identify the Johannine Logos with the "divine logos" of Philo. The latter is not really a person, but only a personification, a figment of the mind construed as the connecting link between the "unknown God" and the world. Because it is a figment of the mind and not a real person, and because the Jewish philosopher constantly wavers between Greek philosophy and the orthodoxy of the Old Testament, his logos has an unstable and indeterminate character. It is even quite impossible to harmonize among themselves the various statements of Philo on the logos. For example, it is hopeless to try to determine to what degree Philo attributes a divine nature to his logos.

What a contrast there is on this point in the plain language of St. John! Although the mysteries he proclaims are incomprehensible and ineffable, the Apostle draws his picture in bold, clear outlines: The Logos is God; He is the only-begotten Son; He became man. It is true that in some expressions there is a shade of resemblance between Philo and St. John, but their utter dissimilarity is so pronounced that some scholars refuse to see in the Apostle's writing even a negation of Philo's teaching. They are of the opinion that either St. John was not acquainted with the logos of Philo, or at least that he does not refer to it at all in his Prologue.

Whatever the case may be, this much is certain: the Johannine notion of the Logos cannot be explained by any of the theories mentioned above. If there is an advantage in seeking a historic basis for the origin of John's idea, then this must be done in the Old Testament or in early Christianity itself.

The opening words of the Prologue have an unmistakable resemblance to the opening words of the Bible: "In the beginning God created heaven and earth." Furthermore, the first pages of Genesis recall repeatedly how God created everything by His word: "And God said, 'Let there be light,' and there was light." Concerning the Logos, who was in the beginning with God, John says: "All things were made through him, and without him was made nothing that has been made." It is also possible that St. John was thinking of the divine Wisdom of the Old Testament which was with Yahweh "before he made anything from the beginning" (Prov. 8:22), and which "is the brightness of eternal light, and the unspotted mirror of God's majesty, and the image of his goodness" (Wis. 7:26). St. John never used the word wisdom (*sophia*); since this word is feminine in gender, it was not suitable to designate the person of Christ. The fact that St. John chose the

71

word logos can more readily be explained as a conscious allusion to the story of creation and the whole tradition of the Old Testament, in which the divine Word plays an important and active role and is frequently represented as a subsistent entity, if not as a distinct person.[7] St. John's choice of the word logos can be readily explained as a development of both Johannine thought and of the primitive Christian mode of expression. For the early Christians, the "word," par excellence, was the glad tidings about Christ, the proclamation of the Christian teaching, the Gospel—not as a lifeless system, but as the power of God: "For the word of God is living and efficient and keener than any two-edged sword, and extending even to the division of soul and spirit, of joints also and of marrow, and a discerner of the thoughts and intentions of the heart" (Hebr. 4:12). "For it [the Gospel] is the power of God unto salvation to everyone who believes, to Jew first and then to Greek" (Rom. 1:16). The preachers of the Gospel are "ministers of the word" (Lk. 1:2) which gives life and salvation. We have already noted that John's Gospel is of a more personal nature than are those of the Synoptics. John focuses all of his attention on

[7] One ought also consider the revelations made by God to His prophets, and also the Law, as "the word of God" and then note that, as Son, Christ is for St. John the adequate revelation of the Father which renders the Law superfluous.

the person of Jesus. The significance of this personality is the theme of the Johannine argument and of
the episodes he recounts. Jesus is Himself the Word,
the divine, efficacious word of creation, the word
of divine revelation, the word of salvation, which
through the Incarnation became light and life for
man. If we recall that the term logos was also used
in the Greek to signify the internal word of the
spirit, we will realize that its application to the pre-
existing Christ is particularly apt.

It is also possible that in choosing the term logos
St. John was influenced by a desire to meet the Greek
mentality. At least in later times ecclesiastical writers
saw in this terminology a point of contact between
Christian doctrine and Greek philosophy. Catholic
theology finds in the Johannine doctrine on the Logos
a profound expression of the eternal generation of
the Son, of that wholly spiritual manner in which the
Son proceeds from the Father. God expresses His
Thought; and this Word, distinct from Him, yet like
unto Him, is His eternal and living image, His only-
begotten Son.[8]

[8] Concerning this point see the recent work of C. H. Dodd,
The Interpretation of the Fourth Gospel, Cambridge University
Press, 1953.

III. The Son

The only-begotten Son—the ineffability of the mystery—the eternal presence—the love of the Father and of the Son—the will of the Father—the mysterious nourishment—Christ's hour.

IN THE life and work of Jesus, throughout His entire existence, as it is portrayed by the fourth Gospel, there is discernible a twofold relationship, one to God and one to man. He is the Son and He is also the Redeemer. This double aspect does not constitute a twofold life in Jesus, but a higher unity. It is precisely as Son, as the Only-begotten who was sent into this world, that He is the Redeemer of the world. All His activity is directed by an ardent passion for the will of the Father; and this will is nothing else than the salvation of the elect through Jesus' complete submission of Himself, even unto death (6:38–39; 3:16 ff.). St. John offers an unexcelled collection of texts treating of the divine Sonship and of the relationship of Jesus to the Father. We are able to choose only a few of them for consideration here.

Christ is the *only-begotten* Son. This one term includes everything, because in John's Gospel it is laden with profound meaning. Reflecting upon the words of the Master, John describes this relationship, as does Jesus Himself, as an intimate union, a bond, which has its central point in Christ, which embraces the totality of His being and extends even to the least of His human activities. The divine Sonship of Jesus possesses an entirely unique character. It is not to be identified with the adoptive sonship of the Christian. The Apostle expresses this unique character by the adjective *only-begotten*.[9] By this term he means the identity of nature and the intimate love which exist between the Father and the Son, which is the efficient source of all divine filiation. The Risen Savior delicately points out this difference between Himself and His brothers, when He says to Mary: "I ascend to my Father and your Father, to my God and your God" (20:17). From this sonship in the strict sense there follows the unity of nature with the Father. Because Jesus chose to assume a passible existence here on earth, He did not permit the radiance of His divine glory to manifest itself prior to His Resurrection (14:28), though it was present throughout His earthly existence and had to be accepted by faith. "I and the Father are one" (10:30; 17:21–23), or as John lets Jesus Himself express it

---

[9] See 1:14, 18; 3:16–18; I 4:9. This term is not used by Jesus Himself, since 3:16–18 is part of a reflection by the writer.

75

in one of His favorite sayings: "The Father is in me and I in the Father" (10:38; 14:10–20). This communion is thus comparable to a mutual penetration, to a perfect reciprocity to each other in knowledge and in love, in their whole life and being.

In God, existence is not distinct from activity, nor thinking from loving. In Him everything is absolute perfection and reality and unity. The spirit of man is not capable of grasping this divine mystery or of expressing it in human language. We can merely try to approximate the mystery of God's nature by multiple thoughts and judgments, which express in part and in a finite manner that infinite perfection which is only one in God. Our images and notions are not equal or adequate to the divine reality: "For we know in part and we prophesy in part: but when that which is perfect has come, that which is imperfect will be done away with" (1 Cor. 13:9). Even John, the inspired contemplative, is no exception to this general law of mankind—this essential limitation of the creature. Jesus adapted Himself to us by speaking our language. Thus we will possibly attain the clearest notion of the mystery of the divine sonship by considering some of the phases of the relationship existing between the Father and Christ. All these aspects are natural consequences of the divine sonship. They are fundamentally expressions of the basic oneness that exists between the Father and the Son.

Thus the fourth Gospel describes Christ's relationships with God as a "being with the Father," as a continuous presence. The Logos was with God (1:1; I 1:2); His Incarnation, His mission into this world, did not bring about a separation: "he [the Father] has not left me alone" (8:29). Even in the uttermost human desolation, even when His trusted friends have fled, Jesus is not alone, "because the Father is with me" (16:32). Jesus Himself admonishes us not to imagine this divine presence as something local or material. It is rather a consciousness of love, an "abiding in love" (15:10). The Other is always there as a loving reality and as the object of enduring love: "And he who sent me is with me; he has not left me alone, because I do always the things that are pleasing to him" (8:29). Jesus often speaks of the intimate mystery of the love of the Father and the Son in the presence of His disciples as well as before others (3:35; 5:20; 10:17; 15:9). "The Father loves the Son." This love is eternal; it fills Jesus with heavenly joy. It is this love and joy which He, the divine-human mediator, transmits to all His disciples and to all true Christians (15:9–11; 17:23–24). The proof of God's overflowing love for the world lies in the fact that He gives

77

"his only-begotten Son" for its redemption. He could not give more, for in doing so He gave Himself (3:16; I 4:9).

The filial love of Jesus corresponds to the Father's love for Him. When He voluntarily accepts a painful death (for "the prince of this world has nothing in him" [14:30]), He does so out of love for the Father: "that the world may know that I love the Father" (14:31). This love of Christ is not merely an affective disposition of the heart. It is a permanent act, an absolute gift, a total submission to the divine will. If there is anything which the Redeemer revealed concerning His personal life, it is this exclusive passion for the will of His Father. On this point the fourth Gospel is in complete accord with the Synoptics. Jesus keeps the commandments, the words of His Father (8:55; 10:18). In His earthly life He accomplishes the work the Father gave Him to do (17:4). He drinks the chalice which the Father gave Him (18:11). When He dies, His last word is: "It is consummated" (19:30).

Perhaps no word of Jesus better expresses this total submission to the will of the Father than His allusion to a mysterious food by which He is nourished (chap. 4). He spoke of it on the evening of the day, when, wearied and hungry after a long journey, He sat down near the well of Jacob. While

His disciples were in the village buying food, a Samaritan woman of questionable moral character came to draw water from the well. In the course of the conversation which ensued, contrary to the customs of the time, Jesus strove zealously for the possession of her soul. In spite of the feminine wiles which the Samaritan employed in order to change the subject, Jesus knew how to win her over and she became His apostle and proclaimed Him to her fellow citizens. Jesus is here engaged in the work of saving souls, the work which the Father gave Him to do (17:4). To this work Jesus gave His all. He had no other reason for existing. When the disciples finally returned with food and invited Him to eat, Jesus did not touch it: "His disciples besought him, saying, 'Rabbi, eat.' But he said to them, 'I have food to eat of which you do not know.' The disciples therefore said to one another, 'Has someone brought him something to eat?' Jesus said to them, 'My food is to do the will of him who sent me, to accomplish his work'" (4:31–34). He lived by the will of his Father. He could not do otherwise than to accomplish this will. To do the will of the Father was as necessary for Jesus as was breathing and eating.

There is yet another series of texts in St. John which strikingly express this union with the will of the Father. Such are the sayings of the Evangelist and also of Jesus Himself concerning His "hour," His "time." The time of Jesus does not coincide, nor can it be synchronized, with that of the world. His life moves in a different pattern. The course of events in the life of the natural man is determined by human calculations and natural necessities. Thus it was the opinion of some of the relatives of Jesus on the occasion of one of the great feasts at Jerusalem that the time had now come for Him to manifest Himself and to present Himself as the Messias. This is a purely human evaluation of events, which tries to determine the opportune moment. But Jesus' time "had not yet come"; not because His calculations had produced a different result, but simply because He was not calculating (7:6–8). His time, the moments for action, all the events of His life, are determined by the will of God, which He sees, and by that will alone. Judging by human standards, how often did He not seem to be hopelessly falling into the clutches of His enemies yet "no one laid hands on him because his hour had not yet come" (7:30; 8:20). And when Jesus knew with the certainty of His divine-human knowledge that "his hour had come, to pass out of this world to the Father," then He surrendered Himself to death with the full power of His love, "loving them to the end" (13:1). This death became for Him the source of the highest glory: ". . . raising his eyes to heaven, he said 'Father, the hour has come! Glorify thy Son, that thy Son may glorify thee' " (17:1).

IV. The Savior

Jesus is the redeemer precisely as Son—the full abundance of redemption—the Good Shepherd—Faith as the way to salvation— the mystery of predestination—Christian salvation in Paul and in the Synoptics—the difference in John's picture of salvation.

JESUS is the Son; He is also the redeemer. It is this latter aspect of His personality which now demands our attention. In Jesus there is no disjunction between Sonship and redemption; He is the redeemer of mankind precisely as Son. Nowhere is this expressed more beautifully than in the fourth Gospel. John describes Jesus' redemptive and saving work as Son as a "being sent by the Father." The earthly existence of Jesus has no other meaning than this mission. For this He came into the world. This is the work which the Father gave Him to do. Repeatedly we find on Jesus' lips the expression "the Father, who has sent me." His consciousness is filled with it; His earthly existence is that of one "who is sent." It is in nowise an existence in Himself or for

81

Himself. These two relationships exhaust each other; He comes from the Father, for mankind, "for the life of the world." St. Paul expressed this same idea, only in other words: "For Christ did not please himself" (Rom. 15:3).

Jesus, the Savior of the world, is the topic of the Gospel. "That believing in him, you may have life." Life here means Christian salvation in its fullness. Thus John sees Jesus as the Savior, who, in His adorable personality, through the revelation of the Father which He is and which He brings to us, grants life through the love with which He surrendered His earthly life. This life He grants in abundance (10:10). "He who has the Son has life" (I 5:12). He is the way, the truth, and the life; the resurrection and the life; He gives the light of life; through Him is grace and truth (14:6; 11:25; 8:12; 1:27). In Jesus is the fullness and abundance of salvation, "the good measure, pressed down, shaken together, running over" (Lk. 6:38). In Him God gives the Spirit without measure as an ever-surging spring, as an overflowing fountain (3:34; 4:14; 7:38).

In the hope that men might ultimately understand, John repeatedly proclaims the comforting truth that Jesus is the Savior of the world. At times He reminds the Jews of their ancient and sacred history: of the manna, the heavenly food; of the bronze serpent which brought healing in the desert (6:26 ff.; 3:14 ff.). But Jesus has more to give than the manna which their fathers enjoyed; He is the "bread of God which comes down from heaven and gives life to the world." Furthermore, He will bring a remedy for every ill, once He has been lifted up above the earth and from the throne of His cross, which is the sign of His glory, once He has drawn all to Himself. Jesus compares Himself to the vine, to that humble wood which sends forth its sweet sap to the farthest branch (15:1 ff.).

Nowhere does He express this more beautifully than in the parable-allegory of the Good Shepherd, the tender yet forceful image of the shepherd and the flock (10:1 ff.) with which Orientals are so familiar. This is not a fanciful idyl, as we sometimes are apt to regard it if we do not understand a shepherd's life in reality, but know it only as it appears in pious pictures. There exists an almost tender intimacy between the shepherd and his charges. Jesus considers this side of the picture; the sheep listen to His voice and He calls them by name, one by one. But there are always the untrustworthy hirelings, the thief, and the wolf, the archenemy of the flock. Because of these enemies a shepherd's existence becomes difficult and sometimes dangerous. But the sheep must be safe; they must live from the bounteous abundance of the green meadows. If necessary the shepherd will even give his life for his defenseless charges. Jesus knows that His sheep cannot live but by His death: "I give my life for my sheep." This acceptance of death is at the same time supreme freedom and supreme obligation. It is a mystery of love. "For this reason my Father loves me, because I lay down my life that I may take it up again. No one takes it from me, but I lay it down of myself. I have the power to lay it down, and I have the power to take it up again. Such is the command I have received from my Father" (10:17–18). Here we encounter the doctrine on Jesus' redemptive death. John rarely speaks of this in his Gospel, and then only in obscure terms.[10] He is clearer in his Epistle; the blood of Christ who died on the cross cleanses us from our sins; He is the propitiation for our sins and for those of the whole world (I 1:7; 2:2; 4:10).

The question is how man shares in this abundant salvation. There is only one way which leads to it: faith in Christ. In his simple, inimitable way the Apostle writes: "He who has the Son has the life. He who has not the Son has not the life." We have the Son by believing the witness that God has given concerning Him (I 5:10–12). To those who believe,

[10] See 1:29; 11:50–53; 12:24f.; 17:19.

He has given the power of becoming children of God (1:12). That mankind can remain blind and deaf in the presence of such a promise of salvation is an incomprehensible and vexing problem. Many, very many, reject the light; they love the esteem of man more than the honor which comes from God (3:19; 12:43). But there are also those who believe, accept, and surrender themselves. John speaks of the latter with joy; he notes the former with profound pain. These are facts which he sees, which he must take into account—but the underlying reasons for these facts are an inscrutable mystery. At times Christ Himself hints at it. They who believe in Him are given Him by the Father. All whom the Father has given Him shall come to Him and He will not reject them; no one can come to Christ unless the Father draws him (6:37 ff.; 10:29; 17:29). One may ask: are not all men given? And how are they guilty, if they do not believe in Christ? And yet they are guilty: "the light has come into the world, yet men have loved the darkness rather than the light, for their works were evil" (3:19). They did not permit themselves to be given to Christ. God called and they did not answer: "Everyone who is of the truth hears my voice" (18:37). This is the mystery of divine predestination and of human cooperation, a profound mystery which the word of St. John illumines like a ray of sunlight: "God so loved the world that he gave his only-begotten Son. . . ."

It is evident to everyone who accepts the data of Holy Scripture that the manner in which John describes salvation and the picture which he draws of Christ as Redeemer do not differ basically from the teaching on redemption by the other New Testament writers. It is always the one Christian salvation, the saving of sinful man from the world, "from the midst of this adulterous and sinful generation," a reconciliation with God through the blood of the Crucified, an incorporation into the kingdom of God through faith in Jesus. It is in the first place a redemption, a freeing from evil—and the only evil known to the Christian is sin. The Precursor has already proclaimed it, and the first public preaching of Jesus is fully in accord: Do penance, be converted! The kingdom of God is at hand. How often did Jesus repeat those blessed and promising words: Go in peace, your sins are forgiven you! "He shall save his people from their sins," the angel had announced to Joseph (Mt. 1:21). "To him all the prophets bear witness, that through his name all who believe in him may receive forgiveness of sins," was the proclamation of Peter on the occasion of the first collective baptism of pagans (Acts 10:43). This early Christian concept of redemption, that is, the forgiveness of sins (Eph. 1:7; Col. 1:14), presupposes a vivid and deep consciousness of sin. There is no one who had a more intense experience of man's universal sinfulness, of his impotence, and of his need for salvation—no one who gave a more gripping expression of this fact than did St. Paul, especially in his Epistle to the Romans.

But one may not imagine Christian salvation as something purely negative. It is not only a freeing from evil; it is at the same time and especially a good gift, a renewal, a power, a new and better life. It is the new and abounding justice of which there is question in the Sermon on the Mount. It expresses itself in an all-encompassing love, a spiritual and truly inner devotion which is simultaneously a gift of God, a grace for which the Christian hungers and thirsts. To put it in Paul's own words, it is the *justice* which man can never merit by works, but which he receives because of God's justification, and God justifies the sinner freely. In Christ he becomes a different man, a *new creature;* through Him and in Him man receives a higher principle of life, the Spirit of Christ. He is a child of God even now, but the perfect state of divine sonship will be his only through the glorious resurrection, when God shall be "all in all" for all eternity.

The various aspects of Christian salvation are

made especially clear in the Epistles of St. Paul.[11] The believer lives and dies according to the example of Christ, who by dying put an end to all that is passible and ephemeral and by rising again inaugurated His glorious existence. In like manner the Christian in baptism dies symbolically and mystically to sin and to his former mode of existence, and rises to a new life, a life for God. It is the duty of the baptized person to realize within himself in a conscious and perfect manner this mystical death and this resurrection unto God. He must perfect this realization until it reaches its consummation in heavenly glory. This consummation will be crowned, so to speak, by the resurrection of the body. Thus, according to St. Paul, Christian salvation has a negative and a positive side—and these are correlative. Here on earth Christian salvation possesses an intensely dynamic character, an innate tendency toward continuous development. It reproduces in a symbolic manner Jesus' death and resurrection; to put it in Paul's own words: "a knowledge of him and the power of his resurrection and the fellowship of his sufferings . . ." (Phil. 3:10).

If we compare John's idea of Christian salvation with that of the Synoptics and of St. Paul, we notice

[11] On this point see Grossouw–Schoenberg, *In Christ*, Westminster, Md.: The Newman Press, 1952.

first that he places less emphasis on the negative element of redemption, the forgiveness of sin. In his view, Jesus is more Savior than Redeemer; *life* is a positive perfection. Christ Himself is the fullness of life and light, and "of his fullness we have all received" (1:16). Jesus redeems us from our sins: John does not deny this; indeed he affirms it, but he seldom speaks of it in his Gospel. He mentions it expressly only once in the word of the Baptist concerning the "Lamb of God, who takes away the sins of the world" (1:29). Although the "Preacher of penance" is a prominent figure in the fourth Gospel, his actual message is nonetheless not given. The Apostle does not use the word for penance (*metanoia,* conversion) even once. In the Epistle there is indeed repeated mention of sin and forgiveness of sin, but it is evident that here John is primarily concerned with the problem of the care of souls, a problem of moral and pastoral theology. John does not deny what Paul asserts so emphatically, but he places the accent differently, and this change of accent is indicative of his own personal insight.

It is as though Paul saw the terrifying power of sin, had had personal experience of man's need of redemption, as though he had tested the whole bitter reality in piecemeal fashion from the bottom to the top. The meditative John on the other hand views the need of the cosmos from above, from the glory of union with Christ. He sees sin as something which is lacking, a not-having of the Son, a not-possessing of the light and the life which He is. One might say that only the experience of a living communion with Christ could have opened his eyes to the utter darkness in which man without Christ is submerged. Intimately connected with this idea is the fact that in John's presentation the Christian existence appears less dynamic than it does in Paul's. In the Pauline letters the Christian life is a difficult mastering of sin and the flesh, a never-ending striving after perfection, a continual battle; the image of the Christian soldier is very dear to Paul. In John everything appears more serene; he maintains a peaceful superiority in inviolable possession. The believer enjoys even now eternal life; the true child of God can sin no more! Here again we have a matter of nuances.

To give an example, John clearly distinguishes different grades of perfection in faith (see 2:23 ff.). Indeed in his Epistle, after some astonishing utterances concerning the sinlessness of the children of God, he considers the possibility of sin; in fact he declares that everyone who asserts that he is without sin is a liar (I 1:8 ff.). Actuality, daily experience, compels him to make these concessions, but he concedes only under constraint. His own view is a different one, an absolute one: heaven on earth. There is yet another difference between John and the Apostle of the Gentiles. In Paul's view Christian life consists in experiencing, both mystically and morally, the two great mysteries of Jesus' life: His death and resurrection. In Paul's mind, the crucified and risen Lord is the Redeemer. John views salvation as inseparably united to the person of the Logos become man without stressing particular phases of His earthly life. Christ is in His own person the life, which was revealed by the Incarnation and in which faith—taken in the Johannine sense—makes us partakers. "He who has the Son has the life" (I 5:12).

Thus we also observe that John in his teaching on salvation prefers to ponder the unchangeable essence of things rather than their external appearances. Yet in spite of these personal inclinations he remains entirely in accord with the early Christian tradition which was painfully conscious of the tribulations of all creation and of the deep longing for the full glory of the children of God: "Beloved, now we are the children of God, and it has not yet appeared what we shall be. We know that, when he appears, we shall be like to him, for we shall see him just as he is" (I 3:2–3).

V. The Adversaries of Christ

The dramatic character of the fourth Gospel—the Devil—the World—the Jews—John's gradual separation from Judaism.

JOHN is not a Gnostic. Yet his spirit indicates some relationship with what may be called the psychological structure of Gnosticism. These gnostic traits may be found in his view of the general world-picture, consisting for him, as it does, of essentially opposed hierarchies. His view of the history of salvation is depicted as a constant struggle of opposing powers. Opposed to light there is darkness; opposed to life there is death. Likewise the work of redemption is obstructed by the forces of sin. At times these powers appear to be gaining the advantage over those of the light, but they are unquestionably routed at the moment of their seeming triumph.

This viewpoint lends to John's Gospel a certain dramatic character which is noticeable even in the Prologue. There are but few characters. Chief among these is Christ, sent and constantly supported by the Father. With Christ are the disciples, a small and timid group who do not yet appear to know the background and the full implication of the struggle. Against Christ the devil appears as the great antagonist, the "ruler of this world." With him are the earthly powers, the world and the Jews. In an advanced position in the enemy's camp there is Judas, the traitor, who is even numbered among the disciples. John intensifies the drama by underlining at the very beginning of his narration the somber character of Judas: "Yet one of you is a devil" (6:71). The tension is increased by the growing hostility of the Jews.

Reading the Gospel we experience the uncomfortable feeling of a circle closing about Jesus, of an unavoidable fate which must have its way. As Jesus prepares Himself for the last journey to Jerusalem we want to join His fearful disciples as they warn Him: "Rabbi, just now the Jews are seeking to stone thee; and dost thou go there again?" (11:8). The Master goes and the fatal denouement comes ever closer. There is a last and glorious manifestation of His divine power: the resurrection of Lazarus—and "many believed in him" (11:48). But from the events which follow we know that the end has come. The supreme council makes an irrevocable decision (11:45–46). Jesus Himself gives repeated clear indications of His imminent death (12:7, 23 ff.). The triumphal entry into Jerusalem can no longer give rise to illusions (12:12–19). In a final summary, the Evangelist sorrowfully but firmly underlines the

93

guilt of the Jews, which only signifies their rejection of salvation and the earthly failure of Jesus' mission (12:37–50). And then, suddenly, when the climax has been reached and our Lord's destruction is determined, as the end begins to unfold with the celebration of the Last Supper, the tension is shattered as a piece of glass (13:1 ff.). The defeat is not the end; shame is really glory; the cross a throne of majesty. "Jesus knew that the Father had given all things into his hand" and "The prince of the world . . . has nothing in me." The Son stands far above all attacks.

The fourth Gospel thus acknowledges three adversaries of Christ the Savior: a superhuman, a human, and a national factor: the *devil,* the *world,* and the *Jews.*

Of these three the devil [12] is the most outstanding. He is the first, the original evil, the murderer and sinner, "from the very beginning." He is "the prince of this world," and the Jews are called his children because they are spiritually related to him through, and in proportion to, their refusal to believe in Christ. The Jews and the world had within themselves the possibility of good—and the whole drama of the Gospel is found precisely in the spurning of this opportunity—but the devil is fixed in evil, he is

[12] See 6:71; 8:44; 12:31; 13:2; 14:30; 16:11; I 2:13f.; 3:8–12; 5:18f.

the evil one par excellence. In common with Christ, he cannot be placed in the earthly sphere; he is a super-human, an other-worldly being. He possesses even a sort of pre-existence; "from the beginning" (of the existence of the human race) he is the adversary of God. In the fourth Gospel the devil does not actually appear as he does in the Synoptic account of Christ's temptation, but he forms a dark background for the two great crimes against the "light of the world": the betrayal of Judas (6:70; 13:2) and the deicide of the Jews (8:44). John calls him the murderer and the father of lies, because by deception he has brought and continues to bring ruin to mankind. His work is sin, and his domain the world. He is the ruler of this world. But through the coming of Christ and His death on the cross the reign of the evil one has been broken at least in principle; he is already "judged" and is being "cast out." Christ destroyed his work and the believers have overcome him in the power of Christ. In the Apocalypse the Apostle describes the final destruction of Satan at the end of time. It is typical of John that he does not narrate a single dia-bolical possession; he is interested only in the spir-itual and moral activity of the devil.

The second enemy is the world. The word *world* (*kosmos*) is one of John's favorite terms and we again experience the typical Johannine width of application. For him world can mean: the universe (17:5), the earth (6:14 ff.), the human race (4:42), or "the world" that is inimical to God and to Christ. The exact limits are not always clearly discernible. In Greek usage the *kosmos* is the beautiful and well-ordered universe, which has its purpose and meaning within itself. For the Jews it is the whole universe precisely as created by Jahweh, which serves Him and manifests His glory. The specifically early Christian significance of the world is that of unredeemed creation, the world without or opposed to Christ. This idea is developed by both Paul and John.

However, in the most properly Johannine use of the term, the word *world* always has reference to the redemption. It has thus become a soteriological concept. Frequently the term is used in a purely natural meaning as the place of Jesus' redemptive activity: Christ is sent into the world by the Father. Generally, however, the world signifies mankind in its relation to the Savior, in its reaction to God's great act of love which is Christ. The world is not necessarily inimical toward God; a priori one might say it is only miserable and helpless. All the need of mankind, the longing for redemption, is expressed in these words: "God so loved the world that he gave his only begotten Son" for its salvation (3:16 ff.).

In its behalf Christ shed His blood; He, who is its Savior, did not come to judge it, but to save it and to grant it life.[13] Life consists in acknowledging Christ's love (14:31). But the world condemns itself, has already condemned itself, by rejecting the light, by refusing to believe in Christ, by killing Him and persecuting His followers.[14] This terrible decision has already been made, and even at the time John is writing, the word *world* often signifies for him a mankind inimical to Christ, a society to which neither Jesus nor His disciples belong. The term almost becomes an expression for everything opposed to the divine revelation in Christ—it is the mark, the description of an attitude which shuts itself off from the workings of God, which occupies itself solely with this earthly sphere and its operations—"Do not love the world, or the things that are in the world. If anyone loves the world, the love of the Father is not in him; because all that is in the world is the lust of the flesh, and the lust of the eyes, and the pride of life; which is not from the Father, but from the world. And the world with its lust is passing away, but he who does the will of God abides forever" (I 2:15–17).

The world withdraws itself from the influence of

---

[13] See 3:17; 12:47; I 2:2; 4:9, 14.
[14] See 3:18; 9:39; 12:25; 15:18ff.

Christ, and where Christ has been excluded the evil one reigns supreme (I 5:18 ff.). Even the *kosmos* itself is personified and is viewed as the great adversary of Christ which, under the leadership of the prince of the world, also persecutes His Church. There is one word which repeatedly expresses the attitude of the world toward Jesus and His followers; it is the word "to hate."[15] The fact that the world hates the Christians is in John's view a necessary result of the essential estrangement which exists between these two spheres: "Do not be surprised, brethren, if the world hates you" (I 3:13). On the last evening of His earthly existence Christ prepared the disciples for the many persecutions which awaited them: "If the world hates you, know that it has hated me before you. If you were of the world, the world would love what is its own. But because you are not of the world, but I have chosen you out of the world, therefore the world hates you" (15:18 ff.).

Because the words of Jesus are based not on accidental facts but on the very essence of things, they have absolute value for all time. The opposition between the world in the latter sense and Christians is permanent. The followers of Christ have been taken out of this world and have been given a new exist-

[15] See 7:7; 15:18ff.; 7:14; I 3:13.

ence: "We know that we have passed from death to life" (I 3:14). The Church is still in the world, but she has a different fatherland, she already belongs to the "coming age," she has her roots in another life. Likewise the thought and the effort of a true Christian differ entirely from those of the purely natural man. The world feels deeply this difference and reacts with aversion and hatred, just as every being instinctively avoids whatever is foreign to it. For this reason the world murdered Christ and with the same hatred His adversaries shall turn upon all who are connected with Him. But even now—even before the blessed glorification of our weak bodies—we are strong through faith in Him: "In the world you will have affliction. But take courage, I have overcome the world" (16:33); "and this is the victory that overcomes the world, our faith" (I 5:4).

The Jews belong to the world more than any others in St. John's estimation. Here we encounter the same phenomenon noted above concerning the Johannine usage of the word "world." Similarly the term "Jews" is often used by John in the normal signification of the inhabitants of the Palestine of that day, the Jewish people together with their national and religious peculiarities. Together with this signification, however, another is found in many places: the term has become almost equivalent to *hater of Christ,* infidel. John does not say this explicitly, but he suggests it by constantly using the word in a certain connotation. It is the "Jews" who constantly contradict Christ, who "murmur" about His teaching, who time and again plot against His life and finally bring Him to death. They are the eternal enemies of Jesus and of His disciples, who are themselves—in the ordinary sense of the word— Jews. Jesus even refers to the Old Testament as "their Law," the law of the Jews (15:25). But in this sense Jesus is not a Jew.

What precisely does the word "Jew" mean? In its pregnant sense as used by St. John the term signifies the Jew of the anti-Christian polemic, the Jew who bases his claim on Moses and the Scriptures in order to deny faith in Christ. The religious opposition between Jew and Christian has been accentuated since the fall of Jerusalem. It was the Jews who incited the Roman authorities and the masses of heathens against the Christians. As a nation they had confirmed themselves in unbelief. In the opposition of the Jewish leaders during the time of Jesus' life on earth John rightly sees the beginning, the nucleus, of the systematic opposition to the Church in later ages.

This anti-Christian signification of the word "Jew" in St. John is indicative of a more general mental attitude: the fourth Gospel separates itself from Judaism. The relationship between Judaism and Christianity is no longer a problem for John. From its earliest beginnings Christianity was universal in principle. It was not bound to any particular state, people, or race. Actually, however, Jesus did restrict His mission to the Palestinian Jews and He faithfully observed the Law, albeit not according to the excessive strictness of pharisaic observation. Likewise the life of the first Christian community in Jerusalem evolved within the limits of Jewish laws and customs as we are told in the Acts. These narrow limits were first broken by the Hellenistic Jewish Christians through men such as Stephen and Paul. The world-wide and historic significance of St. Paul's life and work is precisely this: he drew significant conclusions from universal principles and actually freed Christianity from the Jewish law. He strove so violently to establish this Christian freedom precisely because he had experienced within himself the transition from the severe observance of the Pharisees to the freedom of the children of God—and not merely because of the stubborn opposition of a number of Jews who had become Christians.[16]

At the time of St. John's writing the battle is over; Judaism is no longer a problem. The break is com-

[16] See Rom. 9:1–5; 2 Cor. 11:22; Phil. 3:4–6.

plete. The fundamental and greatly disputed concepts of the Pauline Epistles such as justification, circumcision, justification through faith or through the works of the Law, no longer play a role in his writings. After three generations of Christians, after the fall of Jerusalem and the destruction of the Jewish state and cult, the Church has freed herself entirely from the clutches of Judaism, in spite of violent opposition and persecution.[17]

[17] In his First Epistle John mentions still another category of adversaries who are destined to play an important role in the history of the Church. These will arise from the Christian community itself and are the heretics who deny the reality of the Incarnation. They are in an applied sense the eternally present Antichrist (I 2:18 ff.; 4:1 ff.).

CHAPTER FOUR

The Christian Existence

❖❖❖❖❖❖❖❖❖

I. The Ontological Basis

*The essential and the accessory—St. John
and Christian self-knowledge—born of God
—the Christian life as a being and a dwell-
ing in God—as communion with God—as
perfect union—God as guest and friend of
the Christian—O Christian, acknowledge
your dignity!*

IN BOTH his Gospel and in his First Epistle St.
John describes nothing more beautifully than the
Christian life, the Christian *mode of existence*. As is
his custom, he investigates this matter deeply. He is
not satisfied with superficialities or with the ordinary
obligations and consequences that follow the Christian mode of life, but he tries constantly to penetrate
to the very heart of the matter, to its most basic
elements. The Apostle consequently stresses the es-

sential character, the ontological aspect, of the question. In his view, Christianity is primarily a different mode of being, a new life, and not merely a law, or a cult, or a definite mentality, or even some sort of disposition. Christianity also consists in all these things, but only in a secondary fashion.

When speaking of Christianity today we are often accustomed to start with these secondary elements, for example, the fulfillment of our church obligations. To be a Christian then means to fulfill one's Easter duty and to attend Mass on Sunday. Some Christians look at the Christian life almost as outsiders and not as children of the household. The children of the household know the Church and its salutary benefits from their own fortunate experience; they do not look upon her as an earthly organization of power or an obstacle to life. Even then, when we reflect on the essence of Christianity, we are frequently inclined—because of the pragmatic outlook common to Western man—to regard the Christian mode of existence as a complex of activities and deeds which more or less determine individual behavior. A Christian mode of existence must undoubtedly manifest itself in one's actions—and St. John reminds us constantly of this fact. But this does not express the deepest foundation of the Christian life. At the root of all action there is a mode of being; all external manifestations of life proceed from an interior principle.

This foundation of the Christian life we call sanctifying grace, a gift of God which transforms us interiorly. Even when considering sanctifying grace, it often happens that, practically speaking, one looks upon it as an exterior, almost an accessory, element. Many even think of it exclusively as "being in a state of grace" as the expression goes, thus giving stress to that particular aspect which one might term its juridical consequence, namely the right to heaven which it gives to the individual. John is acquainted with this aspect of grace also; he calls it "confidence in the day of judgment" (I 4:17). But this is only a consequence of the state of grace, not the essence. St. John, the beloved disciple, can heal us from this superficial manner of looking at things, from this lack of a Catholic consciousness and of a legitimate Christian pride. How does he conceive the Christian life; how does he express this supernatural reality?

In the first place, the Apostle describes our supernatural mode of existence as divine sonship.[1] We have already become acquainted with his use of this phrase. But how deeply he experiences this as a reality within his own soul; with what realism he

---

[1] Texts concerning our divine sonship are: 1:12; 11:52; I 3:1–2,10; 5:2. Texts concerning our being born of God are: 1:13; 3:3–8; I 2:29; 3:1–2,9; 4:7; 5:1,4,18.

105

describes this happiness and especially its source: "to be born of God." St. Paul, too, calls a Christian a child, a son, of God, and far be it from me to lessen the truth or the inherent vitality of this Pauline idea. With St. Paul, too, the state of being sons of God is an interior life which has been given us by the Spirit. But among other things St. Paul often treats of the moral and juridical consequences of this sonship: the sons are free, they are not slaves; they are heirs, they should therefore be animated by filial confidence, not by a servile fear (Rom. 8:16 ff.; Gal. 4:7).

St. John, on the other hand, treats almost exclusively of the source of this sonship, of the new *divine mode of existence* which the Christian receives. We grant that he, too, makes the necessary restrictions: that only One is Son by nature, the Only-begotten, and that it has not yet been revealed what we are to be. But what treasures are we not already carrying in earthen vessels? "We are born of God, and his seed abides in us." Incredible realism! Of all the New Testament writers St. John alone pursues the investigation of the divine sonship of the Christian to its primal source: the fact of his "being born of God." One must, however, take care not to misinterpret this phrase; "being born of God" has nothing carnal about it—and this sharp and immediate contrast of the divine with human generation serves only to strengthen the supernatural realism of the Apostle—: "who were born not of blood, nor of the will of the flesh, nor of the will of man, but of God."

Christ Himself explains this more in detail when He corrects Nicodemus' gross misunderstanding. It is a birth through water and the Spirit; through the Spirit first of all—that divine principle which uses the material element of water in the sacrament of baptism and endows it with divine vitality. The adult person is not entirely passive as he receives this gift, for only "to those who believe in his name, does he give the power of becoming sons of God." But how true it is that this new life is a divine life, that it exists because it is a "being born of God," that it *always remains* a "being born of God." "His seed abides in us." Just as Christ Himself "always lives through God," thus constantly receiving being and life and operation from the Father with whom He is one, so the divine principle of life continually operates in the Christian; there is always that living contact with the divine principle. The Christian existence is nourished from this source. Is it to be marveled at that St. John, who has such an *original,* such a basic and essential view of Christianity, dares to add "that a Christian cannot sin, because he is born of God" (I 3:9)?

With this being born of God which continues forever there begins what St. John terms the "abiding in God," "abiding in Christ." [2] The Apostle employs these simple, almost primitive expressions to describe the supernatural reality of the Christian life: God is in the Christian, just as He is in Christ—He abides in us and we in Him, we abide in Christ and Christ in us. John always conceives the Christian mode of existence as a relationship to the divine persons. It is not something which exists of itself, something which is autonomous; nor is it purely human, a purely psychological factor, a spontaneous impulse of sentiment toward the divine. It is a real existence, a mode of being which exists prior to our experiencing it. It is always an existence in relation to God and to Christ; it is always "a fellowship with the Father and with the Son" (I 1:3), a "having of the Father and of the Son" (I 2:23 ff.), a "being born of God," a "being in God and in Christ." The Christian life is at the same time a sovereign reality and a total dependence. Natural powers are absolutely ineffectual here. Yet how intimate is this gracious relationship. It is a permanent and most personal union with God, a mutual immanence, a reciprocal impenetration: God remains in us, we in Him.

[2] Such texts occur in many places; for example 6:57; 15:4–7; I 2:6,24,27f.; 3:6, 24; 4:16.

To put it differently, through faith Christian existence is a "possessing God," is a treasure that of itself is never to be lost; it is an "association with the
Father and with the Son," an association of life and
love, a mysterious immersion of our innermost being
into the divine stream, invisible and hidden, yet
supremely real, divinely real. It is this reality which
the Apostle had been experiencing for many years
at the time of his writing. Thus, in a word, the Christian is in a state of "perfect unity" (17:20 ff.).
Because of his Christian existence he is already par-
taking in divine immutability, in the peace and quiet
for which his heart yearns. His innermost being is
not disturbed by the changes of time, for the Christian possesses "eternal life." He is elevated above
the essential divisions of the created world, above
being now in one state and now in another, for he
has been taken up into the divine unity: "May they
all be one in us, Father. . . ."

This most intimate relationship between God and
man through grace has as its happy consequence a
constantly enduring presence and a mutual love,
analogous to the eternal and loving union of the
Father and the Son. God dwells simultaneously in
the Christian as Lover and Beloved; He reveals Himself to him as *love*. Both Christ and the Father come
to him and abide in him. Jesus Himself says this in

a beautiful passage of His farewell address: "He who has my commandments and keeps them, he it is who loves me. But he who loves me will be loved by my Father, and I will love him and manifest myself to him. . . . If anyone love me, he will keep my word, and my Father will love him" (14:21–23). These words, so sublime in their simplicity, signify nothing less than the inhabitation of the triune God —an abiding of the divine friend—in the soul of the true Christian. Our love arouses His love, and yet, even the first movement of our love was already a response to His call (I 4:19), which invites us to communion and perfect union with Him.

How intensely the beloved disciple was permitted to contemplate and to experience the very essence of the Christian life! We must keep repeating that John prefers to ignore the accidental aspects of this existence in order to penetrate to its very essence. Christian life is a possessing God, a union with God, a divine life. It is all these things already at the present, in spite of all the misery and changeableness, in spite of the world and of sin. This precious jewel of Christian existence sparkles in the writings of St. John with a splendor which no material contact can obscure, from which no distraction can divert us, to which the hatred of the world can only bring us closer. Even though the exterior man perishes—in

110

fact, precisely *because* he perishes—the inner man is renewed from day to day (2 Cor. 4:16). This is the important lesson which St. John teaches us: to become aware of our Christian existence through prayer and contemplation; to touch upon the essence of the matter; to shake off the dust and ashes of our daily drudgery and of sin, for "God is greater than our heart."

II. Faith and Love

The activity of the Christian life—a return to the essentials—faith as surrender of one- self to Christ—faith, knowledge, seeing— love of neighbor, the one and only com- mandment—the perfection of love.

JOHN'S contemplative spirit dwells with loving attention on the profundity of the essence of a Christian life. In order to describe it he coins new expressions which, with great simplicity, cast a new light on the divine mystery of grace that is within us. We must not suppose that St. John is indifferent to the activity of a Christian life. This contemplative is at the same time an intense pragmatist. He is well aware that all true life manifests itself in activity, that it must be unceasingly active: "He who does not

111

love abides in death" (I 3:14). "He who says that he knows him, and does not keep his commandments, is a liar and the truth is not in him" (I 2:4). Jesus Himself avowed in His Farewell Address that "he who has my commandments and keeps them, he it is who loves me" (14:21).

John speaks about Christ's commandments on different occasions. If we ask ourselves just which commandments he has in mind, we will find that he is speaking of only two—and these two are really only one. An active and benevolent love of neighbor always comes to the fore as the great commandment, as the only commandment, as the epitome of all the commandments. "This is my commandment, that you love one another as I have loved you" (15:12). "And this commandment we have from him: that he who loves God should love his brother also" (I 4:21). There is only one place in which John mentions two commandments, and even then he views them as one: "And this is his commandment, that we should believe in the name of his Son Jesus Christ, and love one another" (I 3:23). Faith in Jesus Christ and love of neighbor are prescribed as one commandment.

John desires an intensely active Christianity. But even in this concrete and visible world he simplifies matters, and in conformity with his whole mental outlook he focuses all his attention on this one principal point. His readers also must attend to the essential in this matter; their interest must be deepened, not broadened. The idea that the whole of Christian life can be in practice reduced to the complete exercise of love for one's neighbor is not a new one. Paul had already expressly stated it (Rom. 13:8). If we read Paul's letters carefully, we will find there frequent exhortations to the practice of a multitude of virtues. John however stresses only one idea; in his view the whole of Christian morality is contained in the love of neighbor. However, together with this stress on love, there is frequently also an emphasis on faith in Christ, especially in the Gospel.

We have already observed that it is precisely John's intention in writing to lead his readers to a more profound savoring of their faith. Faith and love—that is the order of activity in John's view of Christianity; it is man's answer to the gift of the heavenly Father. It is faith and love which constitute both the privilege and the fruit of man's divine sonship, of his "being in Him." By faith is meant the complete surrender of the human spirit to the revelation of God in Christ. Love is only the blossoming of this Christian existence as it manifests itself in its relation with other men, considered especially as brothers in Christ.

Faith is one of those concepts, or better, truths, which we in our day have greatly minimized, from which we have drained all active and personal content. In the ordinary language of the day faith has almost become an "objective" notion, utterly impersonal, and entirely rational. It is an intellectual acceptance of a certain system of thought. In practice it has become equivalent to "not being a heretic." As the common expression has it, one believes more or less what is in the catechism and what the Church tells us must be believed. Generally, there is no further intellectual interest in the matter. Even in the majority of theological textbooks the notion of faith is separated from the person of Christ. John views faith differently, and not only John but Paul too; indeed, the whole New Testament has a richer and more appealing idea of faith in Christ than that to which we are accustomed. This faith demands a real surrender of the whole personality; on this faith depends one's ultimate destiny. "He who believes in him is not judged; but he who does not believe is already judged" (3:18). John is acquainted too, with the idea of imperfect faith, the beginning of conversion to Christ, which still relies to a great extent on things external (2:23; 4:28); but true faith, genuine

114

faith, brings with it complete surrender of the entire personality to the person of Christ.

In addition, this faith contains a strong intellectual element, if one wishes to call it that. Jesus constantly returns to this point in the fourth Gospel; the Jews must believe that "he is," that "the Father has sent him." But this intellectual acceptance, even when moved by the will under the influence of grace, does not exhaust the full concept of Johannine faith. It contains much more. It also includes confidence, loving submission, total experiencing, absolute surrender to Christ. It takes hold of the entire person and mobilizes all his forces. Whoever believes in this manner "has life everlasting" (6:47), and we are well aware what John means by that phrase.

This faith, "which works through charity" (Gal. 5:6) and is constantly nourished by prayer and contemplation, is not restricted to mere acceptance of the truth, even when we look upon it primarily as supernatural knowledge. In virtue of the light which irradiates from Christ it grows into a loving penetration of divine truth, to a loving tasting and experiencing of "how sweet the Lord is." Such a love is no longer a mere acceptance on authority of things which remain foreign to us, but it becomes, as John again puts it so simply, a *knowing* through experience; in a certain sense it becomes a *seeing,* a *con-*

templating. And although in the teaching of both St. Paul and St. John immediate and blissful contemplation of the divine essence is reserved for heaven, nevertheless there is possible, even here on earth, in the darkness of faith, a certain contemplation which is given to those who truly belong to Christ. It is given, St. Paul expresses it, to those who "have crucified their flesh with its passions and desires" (Gal. 5:24).

This is what Jesus told the Apostles at the Last Supper: "Yet a little while and the world no longer sees me. But you see me, for I live and you shall live. In that day you will know that I am in my Father, and you in me, and I in you" (14:19–20). As is his wont, John here plays upon the different significations of the word "to see." At the moment at which Jesus is speaking the world still "sees" Him with the eyes of the body. This manner of seeing will cease of itself with His death, and the world cannot see Him in any other way. But the Apostles will see Him even after His death. Does Jesus refer here to His apparitions after His resurrection? Surely not exclusively; the disciples will also see Him in a spiritual manner, just as "his life and their life"—which is the reason of their seeing—is a communion of the divine life. Jesus has in mind the deep and intimate contemplation of faith which shall be their portion when He sends the Holy Spirit after His death. St. John speaks of a similar seeing when he says: "We have seen his glory." This seeing is the perfect faith in the eternally living Christ, which the Apostle desires for all his readers: "He who believes in the Son of God has the testimony of God in himself" (I 5:10).

If faith is thus the basic attitude of the soul toward Christ, the Light of the World, love is the activity of every day and hour.[3] In His last talk to His Apostles Jesus bequeathed the commandment of brotherly love as His spiritual testament to the little flock of His disciples: "A new commandment I give you, that you love one another. By this will all men know that you are my disciples, if you have love one for another" (13:34–35). This was the only power, the only weapon, with which these weak men were to overcome the world—and they did overcome it. The legend concerning the last utterances of the aged Apostle is well known. St. John constantly repeated the one theme: "My little children, love one another." He kept repeating this one sentence in spite of protest, because, as he explained it, that was sufficient. Having read the Epistle of St. John, we know that this account is true in a higher sense. In his opinion brotherly love embraced everything. "Be-

[3] The principal texts in this regard are: 13:34; 15:12, 17; I 2:7–11; 3:11–24; 4:7–21. See also the texts cited under the heading LOVE, pp. 41 ff.

117

loved, let us love one another, for love is from God. And everyone who loves is born of God, and knows God. He who does not love does not know God, for God is love" (I 4:7–8). In his view, brotherly love is surety for everything: for the love of God (4:19–21), for the true *Gnosis* (I 4:7–8), for union with God (I 4:12–13), for the *state of grace* (I 3:14), and for tranquillity of conscience (I 3:19–20). It is the basis for supreme confidence, it banishes all fear (I 4:17–18). Whoever loves his brother may be sure of his union with the Father and the Son. This love satisfies the desire for a certainty of our union with God, for the heaven on earth, of which the whole Epistle speaks. It is the great renewal which Christianity has brought into the world (I 2:7–11).

However, one must be well aware that St. John does not conceive brotherly love as something negative, as a mere abstention from sin. For him it is a positive perfection, a fullness of both disposition and action, which must govern all man's activity—his thoughts and hidden desires, his use of money and possessions, and even life itself. "He has laid down his life for us; and we likewise ought to lay down our life for the brethren" (I 3:16). In a manner that reminds us of the Sermon on the Mount (Mt. 5:21–22) John pursues the lack of love, which in fact constitutes hatred, to the inmost recesses of the human heart (I 3:12–15). He knows that envy is the root of hatred. It was the sin of Cain. "Everyone who hates his brother is a murderer" (I 3:15). Fratricide is the logical consummation of hatred of one's brother; it is its normal consequence. But we refuse to acknowledge this, much less have we the courage to perform it. To the Christian who does not love his brother the Apostle holds up the odious mirror of Cain so that he might see himself in it and be stricken with horror at the vision of his true inner self.

III. Hierarchy and Sacraments

John's individualism—mysticism and ecclesiastical authority—bonds of unity through fraternal charity—personal piety and the sacramental system.

HAVING read the preceding chapters, one might conclude that John looks upon Christian existence as something almost exclusively individual and subjective. Christianity appears to be an affair only of the individual; it unfolds itself within the innermost sanctuary of the soul and exists only between the soul and God. It must be admitted that John does grant full play to the interior and personal element of religion. Because of a strong personal disposition he is much more inclined to this than are the Synoptics. One can scarcely expect anything else from one who wants to preach a more profound Christianity to a later generation. Hence it is typical of John to substitute the more personal concept of "eternal life" for the "kingdom of God" which is the principal theme of the Synoptics and connotes a communal existence. The numerous parables recorded by the three older Evangelists, with which Jesus teaches His hearers and clarifies the nature, conditions, and properties of the Christian society He founded hardly have a parallel in the fourth Gospel. One may think of the allegory of the vine in Chapter 15; but even there the emphasis is on the necessity of individual union with Christ as the condition of a fruitful apostolate rather than on the idea of community, as presented in the parable of the mustard seed, the cockle in the wheat, and many others. Neither is the term *Church* to be found in the fourth Gospel or in the Epistle; the college of the Twelve is frequently referred to as "The Disciples."

This Christian individualism reaches its zenith in the First Epistle. The Apostle warns his readers of the dangers of a sinister error, which strikes at the very basis of Christianity by denying the reality of the Incarnation, and which is being spread by teachers who have their origin in the Christian community itself. It is hardly necessary that he warn them: "But you have an anointing from the Holy One [the internal illuminating grace of the Spirit] and you know all things. I have not written to you as to those who do not know the truth, but as to those who know it, and because no lie is of the truth. . . . As for you, let the anointing which you have received from him, dwell in you, and you have no need that anyone teach you" (I 2:20–21,27).

The Reformers in times past based themselves on these texts in their struggle for the so-called Christian freedom against the ecclesiastical teaching authority. In their view the Christian with his anointing of the Spirit, the interior enlightening which is given him by God, is sufficient unto himself; he is in a position to determine for himself what constitutes truth, and what constitutes error. "You have no need that anyone teach you" (I 2:27). This understanding of the texts, as though they excluded ecclesiastical teaching authority, has its source in a complete misunderstanding of the peculiarities of John's style. The Apostle is wont simply to place side by side the various aspects of a complex problem even when these are diametrically opposed to each other; or better, he expresses them one after the other without establishing a formal connection between them, without weakening them by those cautious formulations to which we are so accustomed. Consequently, if one takes such a sentence out of its context, he has a clause which is apparently absolute, but which actually portrays only half of John's thought.

Such is precisely the case with the point in question. John wants to say that Christians will be protected from the dangers of perfidious error if, listening to the inner voice of the Master, they hold fast to the teaching authority of the Church. Both factors are important; they complement each other. Only he listens as he ought to the voice of both the teaching authority of the Church and of tradition who lets himself be led by the Spirit of God, who properly possesses the internal organ of a Christian instinct, who, one might almost say, has a spiritual relationship with revealed truth. John takes account of both elements, but, as is his custom, in an isolated and, to all appearances, absolute manner. This fidelity to tradition and to ecclesiastical authority is noted expressly in the same passage as that of the anointing of the spirit: "As for you, let that which you have heard from the beginning abide in you. If that abides in you which you have heard from the beginning, you will also abide in the Son and in the Father" (I 2:24). John is, above all, the herald of a personal religion. God instructs the true Christian directly without the voice of man, without external intervention. With this teaching John continues a great tradition; he repeats a thought which the Master himself had expressed: "It is written in the prophets, 'And they all shall be taught of God.' Everyone who has listened to the Father, and has learned, comes to me" (6:45).

The prophets whom Jesus had in mind are Isaias and Jeremias, especially the latter. It was he who dreamed of a glorious new covenant between God and His people: "But this shall be the covenant that I will make with the house of Israel, after those days, saith the Lord: I will give my law in their bowels, and I will write it in their hearts: and I will be their God, and they shall be my people. And they shall teach no more every man his neighbor, and every man his brother, saying: Know the Lord; for all shall know me from the least of them even to the greatest, saith the Lord: for I will forgive their iniquity, and I will remember their sin no more" (Jer. 31:33–34; cpr. Hebr. 8:10–12). However this interior hearing does not exclude the preaching of the faith. This individualism finds its limits, which are at the same time the surety of its genuineness, its infallible protection against self-deception, in humble subjection to the divinely instituted authority: "He who knows God listens to us [*us,* i.e., to John

123

himself with the fullness of his apostolic authority].
He who is not of God does not listen to us. By this
we know the spirit of truth and the spirit of error"
(I 4:6). This is merely the Johannine echo of what
had already been asserted by the Synoptics: "Who
hears you, hears me." For this great mystic, for this
inspired man of God, a simple and humble obedience
to ecclesiastical teaching authority is the decisive
element in determining the true nature of the spirits.

In similar fashion, illusory outbursts of personal
piety are prevented by the sane demands of a prac-
tical fraternal charity. It is sufficient here to refer to
the earlier explanation of charity, especially fraternal
charity. According to John, the continuous bondage
to the community, the ministering to the needs of
one's fellow man, is the best and most genuine of
all religions.

John also fully recognizes the objective, the extra-
personal value in the order of sanctification. His
Christianity is not a vague and ultimately inhuman
spiritualism; it is not some Gnostic immaterialism.
It follows wholly and entirely from the Incarnation
. . . "The Word was made flesh." This mysterious,
but real, union of the divine with the human and
material is continued in the Christian life. None
among the writers of the New Testament stresses
the necessity of the two great sacraments of baptism

and the Eucharist, as does John. He is in a position to do so, because at the time that he is writing the Christians have already been long acquainted with the sacramental practice. This is why he can omit the account of the institution of the Eucharist, which is already known from the Synoptics and from oral tradition. This is his purpose in recording the "Eucharistic speech" at Capharnaum in which Jesus Himself explains the necessity and the profound meaning of communion. This is also why John recounts the conference with Nicodemus in which the meaning of baptism is outlined briefly but sharply as a birth through water and the Spirit.

"The Word was made flesh." "This is He who came in water and in blood, Jesus Christ; not in water only but in the water and in the blood" (I 5:6). Christ carried the Incarnation through to its very end not only by accepting the testimony of God by His baptism in the Jordan but also by submitting to the shame of a bloody death on the cross.[4] He was not ashamed of the flesh. The Word has bound the salvation of the Christian to material things. This necessity obliged even the Gnostic of John's time, who hated matter so much. "Amen, amen, I say to

---

[4] At the same time water and blood are the symbols of baptism and the Eucharist, the two sacraments of initiation into Christianity. In this connection one may also consult the commentaries of the Fathers on John 19:34.

125

thee, unless a man be born again of water and the Spirit, he cannot enter into the Kingdom of God" (3:5). "Amen, amen, I say to you, unless you eat the flesh of the Son of man, and drink his blood, you shall not have life in you" (6:53). In the fourth Gospel the most affirmative and mystic expressions of Christian existence, such as were noted above, are placed side by side with unsurpassed and most expressive terms of the sacrament. "He who eats my flesh and drinks my blood has life everlasting and I will raise him up on the last day. . . . He who eats my flesh and drinks my blood, abides in me and I in him. As the living Father has sent me, and as I live because of the Father, so he who eats me, he also shall live because of me" (6:55 ff.). It is John, too, who has handed down the words of the risen Savior bestowing the power to forgive sins upon the Apostles: "Receive the Holy Spirit; whose sins you shall forgive, they are forgiven them; and whose sins you shall retain, they are retained" (20:22 ff.). Perhaps the word "anointing" in the Epistle, which certainly means the Holy Spirit and His grace, also contains a reference to the sacrament of confirmation. In any case, the strong personal Christianity of John is firmly rooted in the sacramental system.

The beloved disciple, who, as no other, knows the free movement of the Spirit and the inexpressible delights of the interior life of love, knows also the apostolic authority in God's Church to which the life of the soul has been bound by the will of God Himself: "He who knows God listens to us. . . ." He knows that there is one—though he be not a poet, a philosopher, a hero, or not yet even a saint, but a living and an honest man—who is constituted by Christ as the shepherd of all the lambs and the sheep (21:15–17). But the last and perhaps the best which we retain from this severe yet tender mystic is the insistent law of charity toward our fellow man *in the concrete,* toward our neighbor whom God has set upon our way, toward the other man we meet on the street, or in the home, or in any other place, whether today, tomorrow or at any time. . . .

Index of Scripture Texts*

* Bold face page numbers indicate that the text is quoted more or less in full on those pages.

INDEX

A NOTE ON THE TYPE
IN WHICH THIS BOOK WAS SET

This book is set in Intertype Garamond, a type face considered by many as one of the most successful ever introduced. Claude Garamond, the designer of these beautiful types, was a pupil of Goeffroy Tory, a leader of the Renaissance in France, a university professor, artist, designer and printer who set out to place French on an equal footing with Latin and Greek as a language of culture. Garamond's evenness of color throughout the font is highly appreciated by book designers. The moderately strong fine lines tend to soften the effect, which is decidedly agreeable to many. One thing is certain, Garamond is unusually pleasing and will distinguish much good printing for many years to come. This book composed by York Composition Co., Inc., of York, Pa., and bound by Moore & Company of Baltimore. The typography and design of this book are by Howard N. King.